The DYNAMICS *of* POLITICAL CRIME

Jeffrey Ian Ross
University of Baltimore

SAGE Publications
International Educational and Professional Publisher
Thousand Oaks ▪ London ▪ New Delhi

For information:

Sage Publications, Inc.
2455 Teller Road
Thousand Oaks, California 91320
E-mail: order@sagepub.com

Sage Publications Ltd.
6 Bonhill Street
London EC2A 4PU
United Kingdom

Sage Publications India Pvt. Ltd.
M-32 Market
Greater Kailash I
New Delhi 110 048 India

Printed in the United States of America

Library of Congress Cataloging-in-Publication Data

Ross, Jeffrey Ian.
The dynamics of political crime / by Jeffrey Ian Ross.
p. cm.
Includes bibliographical references and index.
ISBN 0-8039-7044-7 (cloth) — ISBN 0-8039-7045-5 (paper)
1. Political crimes and offenses. 2. Political corruption.
3. Political persecution. I. Title.
HV6273 .R67 2003
364.I'32—dc21

2002007523

02 03 04 10 9 8 7 6 5 4 3 2 1

Acquiring Editor:	Jerry Westby
Editorial Assistant:	Vonessa Vondera
Production Editor:	Diana E. Axelsen
Copy Editor:	Kris Bergstad
Typesetter:	C&M Digitals (P) Ltd
Cover Designer:	Ravi Balasuriya

CONTENTS

FOREWORD

Kenneth D. Tunnell

———•••———

A s I wrote this foreword to *The Dynamics of Political Crime* on July 1, 2002, news coverage was on the immediate future—the first July 4th since that fateful day of September 11, 2001, when terrorists used passenger planes as weapons to attack the World Trade Center in New York City and the Pentagon in Washington, D.C. Newscasters, with wrinkled brows and just the right touch of concern in their voices, frequently (nearly hourly) reminded us of vague terrorist threats and possible violent scenarios. New York's mayor publically encouraged city residents to "get out" and celebrate July 4th festivities, because "otherwise, the terrorists will have won." The country is at war; indeed war, has been declared on a state-less yet internationally operative terrorist organization known as al Qaeda. Ironically, while the United States galvanizes war efforts around the world, captives are treated as something other than prisoners of war, meaning international conventions and treaties governing such prisoners are inapplicable. The president and talk radio dismiss terrorists as "evil." Yet, we gain little understanding of those terrorists and their activities from such a dismissal. Worldwide, learned men and women (especially the intelligentsia) situate those terrorists within political explanations. And although there is disagreement on the specifics of the terrorists' motives, one paramount explanation is that they and their organizations are engaged in political crimes. Failure (or perhaps refusal) to abide by the Geneva Convention (which governs the treatment of prisoners of war) is not defined publically as political crime.

The ability to treat the other's actions as crime (whether street crime or political crime) begins with power. The ability to evade having the criminal label applied to oneself likewise depends on power. The United States—indeed, most of the world—regards al Qaeda as a terrorist organization possessing an organizational subculture and goals and strategies. The United States (and some of the world) treats particular countries as terrorist states or at least states that sponsor terrorism. Yet, definitions of terrorism are dynamic; as a result, nations (and organizations) defined as terrorist change over time. Across the globe, countries (and especially world powers), regardless of their current or historical behaviors, are able to ignore attempts to treat them and their actions as terrorist. Power and rhetoric typically are inseparable mechanisms by which the other is defined as political criminal. This same argument is central to the white-collar crime literature, which suggests that the law (and the administration of legitimate force) is biased in a particular direction—in favor of the powerful over the less powerful. As a result, misdeeds among the privileged classes typically are excluded from criminal definitions, while illegitimate behavior among the less affluent is widely considered deviant and in many cases, criminal. The similarity in the place of power for determining who is and who is not a political criminal is striking.

The Dynamics of Political Crime highlights the complexity in labeling countries, and especially those very powerful ones, as either terrorists or political criminals and the ease and processes by which dissidents, protestors, and anti-systemic organizations are labeled as such. Groups and individuals revealing a country's misdeeds or anti-systemic confederations attempting to fundamentally alter a country's identity, always, by design, find themselves facing insurmountable institutional strictures. And often, they find that they themselves are the ones who are publically treated as political criminals engaged in political activities that are re-cast as political crimes.

This scenario reminds me of other hot, humid, July days just a few short decades ago. The historical events from that time stand out in my mind and undoubtedly in those of many of the baby boom generation. Then, too, the United States was engaged in a conflict, one that also was far from home (in Vietnam). Indeed that war became the single event that ignited the country in various political actions, some of which were treated as political acts and political crimes. But, there were other salient events during those times: the civil rights movement; assassinations; the free speech movement; and federal agencies spying on U.S. citizens because of their political ideology and affiliations.

Cities burned. Watts (in Los Angeles), Detroit, Chicago. Attempts were made by rebellious students to commandeer universities and occupy administration offices. In response, troops were called in, and in some places students were killed. We cannot ignore the reality that each of these acts was political. Many of these events violated international standards of human rights. Some were prosecuted as political crimes. Others were prosecuted as criminal behavior. Still others were upheld by law. In the main, and simply put, dissidents and anti-systemic groups were treated as criminals by the state with little attention given to the politics of their behaviors. Efforts made to label the state and its agents as political criminals met with little success. Since that time, changes have occurred in the public psyche, in social control strategies, and in surveillance and spying modalities. Most important, though, cultural changes have occurred so that today, with the exception of the Los Angeles riots during the early 1990s and the occasional political demonstration, these types of events are rare occurrences.

Students and the general public normally don't think of states or political leaders and their operatives as criminal. Using a strictly legal definition, they rarely are. Yet, they sometimes do engage in unlawful behavior, such as rigging or manipulating elections (which, in a democracy, is considered a serious offense); spying on, kidnapping, and torturing oppositional forces; or accepting bribes. Such activities typically violate those countries' own domestic laws. Beyond legalistic definitions, states and their agents also ignore international rules, procedures, and basic human rights. Defining states' activities as political crimes and states and their operatives as political criminals is a difficult task, in part because such activities are organizational in nature. Organizational political crimes, as detailed in *The Dynamics of Political Crime,* are those that transcend the responsibility of any one single individual; rather, the organization itself assumes the illegitimate practices as a part of its everyday behavior. In other words, illegitimacy becomes the organization's standard operating procedure. It trickles down through various offices and touches various office holders; it is made possible by the hierarchical nature of work in that one single office only contributes to the ideology or practice while another office, perhaps isolated from the former, also contributes to it, and on down the line. As a result, no single individual or office can be held completely responsible; there typically is no "smoking gun." This presents difficulties for establishing responsibility, and without someone, somewhere being accused, the criminal label is difficult to apply. Such is the case with both political and corporate crimes. This book highlights these difficulties and suggests some responses for teasing out the processes by which responsibility can be assigned.

In the main, *The Dynamics of Political Crime* takes us on a journey that illuminates the different types of political crimes and the means by which they are defined. It further highlights theoretical explanations by focusing on both organizational and individual issues; in other words, both structure and agency receive attention as each is heralded as a worthwhile theoretical explanation. Also relevant is the issue of political crimes committed by states and those committed by individuals and groups engaged in oppositional crimes (e.g., anti-systemic). As a result, *The Dynamics of Political Crime* is a holistic and balanced account of the features of political crime as it is treated within the social sciences.

PREFACE

———•—•———

Nearly three decades ago, I dropped out of high school and, for close to 5 years, bounced around a number of "working-class" jobs. My last "adventure" was driving a cab. I did this for 2 years before I decided to enroll in a remedial/bridge course that would enable me to get into college. I was fresh off the streets, but through hard work, determination, and the recommendation of a sympathetic instructor, I managed to get into the University of Toronto (U of T) through a back-door program. It was at U of T that I had the benefit of taking my first course in deviance with Austin T. Turk. His class provided me with an excellent venue that started a long process of consolidating my intuitive thinking about the connections among deviance, crime, and politics.

The Dynamics of Political Crime is the result of this journey, personal, political, and intellectual, that benefited from a series of ongoing discussions with colleagues, policymakers, convicts, ex-cons, and law enforcement personnel, as well as from research and writing I have conducted on various aspects of political crime.

In this process I have learned from many of my colleagues, especially Gregg Barak, Dorothy Bracey, David Charters, Raymond Corrado, Jeff Ferrell, David Friedrichs, Larry Gould, Mike Gunter, Ted Robert Gurr, Donna Hale, Mark Hamm, Leon Hurwitz, Vic Kappeler, David Kauzlarich, David Mason, Otwin Marenin, Rick Matthews, Stephen C. Richards, Ira Sharkansky, Kenneth D. Tunnell, Austin T. Turk, Mike Vaughn, Barbara Yarnold, Michael Welch, Leonard Wienberg, Steve Wright, and others.

Ultimately, dissatisfaction with the existing descriptions and theoretical explanations of political crime, and recognition that the field has changed since the publication of Turk's seminal *Political Criminality* (1982), motivated me to write this book.

Although my work on this project predates the coordinated hijacking and crashing of airliners into the World Trade Center buildings, the Pentagon, and a field in rural Pennsylvania, the events of September 11, 2001, the hours, and the days that have passed since that tragedy have been firmly etched in my mind. I often wonder how those acts compare with other acts of political crime, and if my thoughts concerning this book would have been different had the tragedy not occurred. In all honesty, I'm doubtful that it changes the way political crime takes place or is analyzed.

ACKNOWLEDGMENTS

I am also grateful to a number of people whose support, encouragement, and patience were invaluable during this project: Terry Hendrix, and later Jerry Westby, at Sage Publications, who adopted, guided, and supported this project through its several stages; Vonessa Vondera, also at Sage, for administrative details; my students, who endured various parts of this project as lectures and required readings; Alexander Murray and Cheri Peterson for research assistance; Paul Bond, Morad Eghbal, William McDonald, Bridget Muller, Stephen C. Richards, and Kenneth D. Tunnell, who provided careful reviews of some or all of this manuscript; to the anonymous reviewers who helped me focus my thinking; Diana Axelsen for production matters; Kristin Bergstad for copyediting; and finally to my wife, Natasha J. Cabrera (who filled numerous roles), and my children Keanu and Dakota, who gave me daily encouragement while tolerating my divided attention.

ONE

INTRODUCTION

———•—•———

Political crime is rarely examined when studying the dynamics of crime, justice, and law. Yet understanding political offenses is fundamental to comprehending the workings of a criminal justice system that selectively defines, enforces, and adjudicates what and who are defined as criminal (Kirchheimer, 1961). As a variety of scholars, jurists, policymakers, legislators, and activists have argued, the law and (by extension) crime are political acts. Hence, interpreting law, crime, and criminals requires a political focus (e.g., Allen, 1974; Chambliss, 1976; Chambliss & Seidman, 1982; Quinney, 1970, 1977).[1]

Various criminal acts are explicitly political. For example, sedition and treason have traditionally been viewed by states as political offenses or illegalities[2] because of their real or alleged threats to order (public, social, or otherwise) or national security.[3] As a result, these behaviors have been codified in law.[4] However, some state reactions to dissent are—in some cases—almost or actually criminal, as governments occasionally engage in repressive actions where law-abiding individuals and groups are respectively placed under surveillance, harassed, infiltrated, and destabilized.

These escalating state responses are rarely recognized in domestic law. Both actions—oppositional and state-initiated—are increasingly acknowledged by many scholars and activists as political crime. Likewise, and according to recent theoretical advances in criminology, sociology, political science, and law, many controversial behaviors are considered politically and socially harmful, yet are not presently classified in legal codes as criminal.

1

In order to accommodate changes in current thinking, this analysis recognizes that legal definitions of crime are often too narrow and that law is dynamic. In other words, we cannot impose the kind of neutrality upon the law that might be implicit in the statement, "Equal justice under the law." Thus an alternative, more contemporary, and inclusive definition and conceptualization of crime is needed. One definition that is gaining increasing legitimacy recognizes that crime is not only a type of deviance or a violation of a criminal law, but also can be interpreted by the wider body politic as a social harm, moral transgression, and/or civil or human rights violation (e.g., Bohm, 1993; Schwendinger & Schwendinger, 1975; Sutherland, 1949a, 1949b).[5]

This "social justice" perspective acknowledges that some behaviors are not traditionally labeled criminal, but should be, and that certain activities that do not violate the existing law yet fall under the previously mentioned characteristics should be considered crimes. This notion would accommodate not only the actions of individuals and organizations in conflict with each other, but also states and their employees. Thus political crime is a more far-ranging label than previously considered.

OBSTACLES TO UNDERSTANDING AND INTERPRETING POLITICAL CRIME

It is difficult to come to terms with political crime. Several reasons contribute to this state of affairs. In general, there is often a lack of consensus, good information, analysis, or interest about political crimes. Undoubtedly, there is considerable confusion about what constitutes a political offense. Experts are often divided over how to define political illegalities. It almost appears as if there is a different definition for each theorist. And information presented by the mass media (e.g., movies, books) and news media (e.g., newspaper, radio, television) minimizes the ability of citizens to understand political crimes properly (e.g., Barak, 1994; Warr, 1995).

Although this is less the case with oppositional political crimes (e.g., terrorism), media construction of state crimes (e.g., genocide) often presents them as unavoidable illegalities, or the "just deserts" given to "irrational" dissidents. Perhaps more important, identifying crimes by the state is not popular. Many people do not criticize their own political system's legitimacy because of high levels of trust, deference to authority, apathy, or the repeated experience of powerlessness (e.g., Dionne, 1991; Ross, 2000b, chap. 5). Alternatively, the public rarely engages in political participation because of the interrelated processes of cynicism, skepticism, and complacency. For most people, the principles of universally applied justice and equality before the law remain central to their idea of the criminal justice process. The notion that their own government commits crimes is unthinkable, thus the end result is a citizenry that fails to believe that these political offenses are widespread and deplorable, and that fails to act to right a wrong.

In addition, many academics are slow to incorporate political crime into their research agendas. Thus, rarely do the leading scholarly journals have articles dealing explicitly with political crime. And few books written by professors are published on this subject each year.

Almost two decades ago scholars and students would have been hard-pressed to find an introductory criminology textbook that had a substantial discussion about the role of politics in the creation of crime, much less an entire chapter to the concept of political crime (Morn, 1974, chap. 2). Today, however, most reputable entry-level texts include this material (Tunnell, 1993a). This is not necessarily because there has been an increase in the amount of political crime, but because the subject matter has moved into the mainstream.

Moreover, the higher education curriculum is reluctant to list classes focusing specifically on political offenses. Few criminology and criminal justice departments at colleges and universities offer classes on political crime.

With the exception of terrorism, the wider problem of political crime, as defined as such, does not appear to be a major policy question. And if research funding is an indicator of government and private foundation interest, things are lacking in this area too.

CLARIFYING WHAT POLITICAL CRIME IS

In sum, political crimes consist of

> crimes against the state (violations of law for the purpose of modifying or changing social conditions) . . . [and] crimes by the state, both domestic (violations of law and unethical acts by state officials and agencies whose victimization occurs inside [a particular country]) and international (violations of domestic and international law by state officials and agencies

whose victimization occurs outside the U.S.). (Beirne & Messerschmidt, 1991, p. 240)

Given this categorization, a domestic political crime includes a correctional officer violating a prisoner's civil, human, or constitutional rights here in the United States (Welch, 1996, pp. 342-344). On the other hand, an international illegality would be the destabilization of a foreign government, as the United States was accused of attempting to do in Allende's Chile in 1970 (Agee, 1975). Alternatively, the 1998 bombing of the U.S. embassies in Kenya and Tanzania, allegedly committed by the al Qaeda terrorist organization (followers of Osama bin Laden), would be an international criminal action (Bodansky, 2001; Reeve, 1999, chap. 1).

Jurists usually distinguish a crime by referring to the existing criminal code, and if this is not sufficient, they examine the perpetrators' motives, affiliations, targets/victims, and the effects of the action (e.g., Kooistra, 1985). Thus, what is most important is the notion of context. Context allows us to understand who is the victim, who is the perpetrator, and what kind of harm has been done.

In general, an actor has committed a political crime if he or she has a political or ideological intention or motivation to cause harm. The clearest example of an oppositional political offense is illegally forcing a change or overthrowing the existing government of a country. State political crime consists of an action perpetrated by the government to illegally minimize or eliminate threats to its rule.

Caution, however, is paramount when analyzing political crime, because some kinds of actions are conducted in a political context but not labeled as political crimes. For instance, unless one delves deeply into the psyche of the perpetrator, an assault against a police officer by a protester at a political demonstration, like what may have taken place at recent anti-globalization protests in Seattle, Washington, D.C., and New York City (2000-2001), is not commonly thought of as a political assault. Alternatively, the American-based Black Liberation Army (BLA) and its direct targeting and killing of police officers in New York City during the 1970s is political crime (Bell & Gurr, 1979).

If the intent of the action is in opposition to the state, then the incident is generally considered a political crime. This argument, however, gets slippery in situations where intent is dubious, and when we move to the dilemma of multiple possible interpretations. Take, for example, an engineer who works for an airplane manufacturer that builds a new version of a fighter jet.

In an effort to raise his standard of living or to pay off creditors, he sells the plans of the fighter aircraft and other useful information to a foreign spy. Although he is cognizant of the implications of his actions, he is motivated not because he is opposed to his country's defense policies or practices or because he is in favor of the foreign government; he sells the information for the financial gain he wants or needs. The issue of ideology is absent, but potential harm to the national security of the state is present, so the engineer's actions should be classified as a political rather than a nonpolitical crime. As this example should demonstrate, intent is neither necessary nor sufficient for an action to be labeled a political crime.

To clarify further, some crimes can be identified as political based on the affiliation of the individual. If the person is part of a recognized terrorist organization, then it is highly likely, but not certain, that that person's action had a political intent. (Terrorists, unlike most government employees, don't carry identity cards.) Others, such as Theodore (Ted) Kaczynski, the "Unabomber," did not have an affiliation, but it is clear through his manifestos that his letter bombs and parcels had a political intent.

Alternatively, political crimes also can be identified by the effect of the criminal action on the government and the public. Whether the event is committed against the state or by the government against a citizen, if it results in harm, we can say a political crime has occurred. In this context, the state is the apparatus of government, interests identified with the government, and people who work for the government (i.e., bureaucrats, administrators, politicians) (Carnoy, 1984; Evans, Rueschemeyer, & Skocpol, 1985). In sum, political crime is like that age-old expression, "If it looks like a duck, walks like a duck, and quacks like a duck, then it must be a duck."

Finally, in addition to the unique nature of political crime, the majority of these kinds of offenses are perpetrated by or against the federal government; thus state and local law enforcement agencies are often handmaidens of the policies and practices of federal agencies. Another way of looking at this relationship is that the power of the central state extends from Washington, D.C., to agencies beyond the Potomac River. In sum, you can identify a political crime through triangulating among existing laws, the individual's (or group's) motivations, the kind of victim/target attacked, the result, and the context of the action.

WHY POLITICAL CRIME HAS CHANGED
OVER THE PAST 20 YEARS

Over the two decades since the publication of Turk's seminal book, historical events leading to new policy concerns have affected the nature and response to political crime. Many longstanding threats to national security have disappeared and new ones have developed.[6]

With respect to the United States, in 1990, shortly after the election of Boris Yeltsin, the formerly Communist Soviet Union and many of its satellite countries dissolved into a loose confederation of states. Two years later (February 1, 1992) it was officially acknowledged that the Cold War between the United States and the Soviets had ended. Most of these countries are taking their first steps toward Western-style democracy.

In the early 1990s, it appeared that peace was finally coming to the Middle East. After a decade-long Intifada (a low-intensity resistance by Palestinian youths to the continued Israeli occupation of the West Bank and Gaza), the Palestinian-Israeli (Oslo) peace accords (1993) were signed. For once there was hope and evidence that a democratic Palestinian state was being established that could coexist beside Israel. This historic agreement culminated with Yasser Arafat, leader of the Palestinian Liberation Organization, shaking hands with Israeli Prime Minister Yitzhak Rabin, with President Bill Clinton in attendance, all on the White House lawn. But on November 4, 1995, Rabin was assassinated by an individual opposed to the peace accord and change was slow. By 2001-2002, increased violence on both sides made stability in this relationship look like a remote possibility. In the background, on August 2, 1990, Iraqi tanks crossed the border into Kuwait. An international armed force led by the United States was assembled and successfully pushed the Iraqis back. Although the Persian Gulf Crisis was successful in its intent (with a surrender signed February 24, 1991), Saddam Hussein remains in power as the president of Iraq.

Elsewhere, in February 1994, Bosnian Serbs attacked an open-air market in Sarajevo, unleashing the beginning of a major civil war in the former Yugoslavia, which included war crimes, ethnic cleansing, and genocide. This precipitated a refugee crisis and the involvement of the United Nations forces for most of the past decade.

In 1994, in South Africa, the racist apartheid system ended, and that same year, the country elected Nelson Mandela its first black president; he had been incarcerated for close to 27 years as the leader of the outlawed African National Congress. And in April 1994 in Rwanda, Hutus and Tutsis fought each other, resulting in one of the worst genocides of the past decade.

Charges of state crimes were not limited simply to countries outside of the United States. On March 3, 1991, four white Los Angeles policemen were caught on videotape severely beating African American motorist Rodney King. This led to their suspension and the filing of criminal charges. On April 29, 1992, when the all-white jury in neighboring Simi Valley, California, acquitted the officers, Los Angeles became the scene of a major riot that lasted close to a week. Also in 1992, in Ruby Ridge, Idaho, federal agents tried to arrest avowed white supremacist Randy Weaver on weapons charges. The armed standoff resulted in snipers killing his wife and baby child. In 1993, in Waco, Texas, the Bureau of Alcohol, Tobacco and Firearms (a division of the U.S. Department of the Treasury) tried to arrest David Koresh, the charismatic leader of a Christian millenarian sect called the Branch Davidian. The situation lead to another standoff, at the Davidians' compound. After 51 days, the final assault, led by the FBI, resulted in the place becoming a veritable inferno. Eighty-six cult members, including children, died in the flames. These incidents only served to bolster a fledgling militia movement in the rural West. In January 2001, President Clinton left office under a shroud of controversy because of a number of scandals (Whitewater, abuse of power, and romantic or sexual involvement with assorted women) he (and sometimes his wife) was involved in.

Moreover, technology (especially information and electronic) has improved and is now widely used, increasing the ability of both oppositional and state actors to engage in political crimes (e.g., Ackroyd, Margolis, Rosenhead, & Shallice, 1980). Furthermore, many of the major incidents and perpetrators of state crime have been recognized by the public and scholars alike. Work has begun in South Africa with the "Truth Commission," and in Rwanda, Bosnia-Herzegovina, and through the world court in The Hague, Netherlands, to bring perpetrators of genocide, human rights violations, and war crimes to justice.

In addition, arguably the best-known type of political crime—terrorism—has increased in many countries. During the past decade alone, on U.S. soil, we have seen some of the most dramatic acts. On February 26, 1993, members of al Qaeda placed a truck bomb in the underground parking garage of the World Trade Center (WTC) in New York City. Although the bombers' original intent was to fell one of the buildings, the resultant blast killed 6 people and injured 1,042. On April 19, 1995, in Oklahoma City, decorated military veteran Timothy McVeigh, along with Terry L. Nichols, detonated a bomb in a Ryder truck that destroyed the Alfred P. Murrah Federal Building. One hundred sixty-eight people were killed, including several children in the building's second-floor day care center. McVeigh, who was later apprehended and given the death penalty, said that he committed the action because of his disappointment with the federal government in the Ruby Ridge and Branch Davidian incidents. On April 3, 1996, Theodore (Ted) Kaczynski (known as the Unabomber) was finally arrested and charged with a series of mail bombings he had perpetrated that were ostensibly directed against supporters of technology and who were hurting the environment. Then on September 11, 2001, not satisfied with their original mission, al Qaeda members hijacked four airplanes and plowed two of them into the two towers of the WTC, one into the Pentagon, and one into a rural field in Pennsylvania. This act alone probably stands as the most dramatic incident of terrorism. On March 20, 1995, Aum Shinrikyo, a religious cult operating in Japan, released sarin, a deadly nerve gas, in Tokyo's subway system. This resulted in the death of 10 people and injury to more than 5,000. And in the fall of 2001 a number of deadly anthrax-filled letters were sent through U.S. post offices, some addressed to well-known television broadcasters and others to politicians. The attacks led to the deaths of three people, hospitalization of others, and the slowdown and virtual shutdown of the U.S. postal system.

In sum, over the past 20 years, the world, the players, and technology have changed, and this has implications for the study and response to political crime.

TYPOLOGIES AND CATEGORIES OF POLITICAL CRIME

Two major distinctions are important in the study of political crime: targets and perpetrators.

Targets

Although a variety of specific types of political crimes are covered in different sections of this book, they can be classified into two types: oppositional (or anti-systemic) and state (or pro-systemic). The former refers to those actions committed by individuals, groups, and countries that want to change or dismantle a particular political or economic system, its institutions, the state, and/or interests aligned with it (e.g., major corporations).[7] The latter types of political crime encompass those actions committed by the state's criminogenic agencies (e.g., police, military, and national security agencies), including their managers and agents, against their own citizens, foreigners, or their governments (Roebuck & Weeber, 1978; Ross, 1995/2000, chap. 1; Ross, 2000d).

Generally, research on political crime does not accommodate both types of crime or link them together. However, in order to understand thoroughly the full scope of political crime, it is necessary to appreciate the interdependency (both conceptual and substantive) of oppositional and state political crime.

Perpetrators

Various categories of political criminals (or perpetrators) (e.g., organizational, occupational, and individual) also exist (Roebuck & Weeber, 1978, pp. 7-8). The first type, organizational, refers to situations where crimes are committed on behalf of, or for, a collection of people who are part of a particular unit, whether that is a terrorist group or a national security agency.

The second category, occupational, encompasses particular crimes committed by individuals in the course of their jobs for their own personal gain, both pecuniary and nonpecuniary (e.g., corruption).[8] Some jobs are structured such that individuals performing them are often put in situations where they occasionally must break the law in order to achieve the goals of the organization.

Lastly, some political crimes are committed solely by individuals acting independently, occur without any organizational involvement or support, and benefit only the perpetrators participating in such misdeeds.

Furthermore, political criminals often do not define their actions as illegal. They minimize conceptualizations of themselves as criminal through complicated mechanisms of denial, rationalization, and neutralization (Sykes & Matza, 1957). These mental processes allow individuals to justify their violation of the law or of other norms, and negate any impression of themselves as criminals. Individuals can rationalize their behavior before and after the deviant act (Coleman, 1994, p. 202).

Why Is This Distinction Important?

Political crime, in general, is also dependent on the tensions among people, occupations, and organizations. For instance, the problem of mobilizing appropriate resources to organizational breaches is an important problem for many administrative settings. Individual terrorists, for example, may not want to wait for the group they belong to or with which they share sympathies to reach a consensus before taking political action.

The difference between organizational, occupational, and individually based political criminals is fundamental to any discussion of political crime that attempts to understand the various causes and effects of political crime. Organizationally based crimes are potentially much more egregious than occupational and individual crimes. Put simply, groups can marshal more resources and thus have a greater detrimental or adverse impact on civil rights, personal liberties, freedoms, and lives than individuals.

Where Does State Crime Fit In?

Although democratic governments and their employees are bound by specific laws and statutes forbidding them to engage in illegalities (typically embedded in criminal and administrative law), they periodically violate these rules for particular purposes.

Crimes committed by the state are somewhat unique because they include illegalities committed by the government as a whole, by organizational units of the state, and by individual officials who break the law for their own personal or their agency's gain (Ross, 1995/2000; Ross, 2000c). These types of crime differ because the former is organizationally based whereas the latter is regarded as individual crimes of occupational corruption. Just as some types of white-collar crime are organizationally based (e.g., the Ford Pinto case of violence against consumers; e.g., Cullen, Maakestad, & Cavender, 1987), some specific political state crimes are also considered organizational (e.g., Kauzlarich & Kramer, 1993, 1998). For instance, the FBI's ongoing illegal surveillance of American citizens (1925-1972; see Chapter 7, this volume) was an agency-wide operation, conducted with the guidance of top FBI officials, and involved almost every field office in the United States (Churchill & Vander Wall, 1990; Davis, 1992). Finally, these actions should not necessarily be viewed as conspiracies where government actors (managers and bureaucrats) secretly and systematically plan and commit crimes, but as unsavory outcomes of organizational goals and constraints (Parenti, 1995, chap. 8).

WHAT THIS BOOK ATTEMPTS TO ACCOMPLISH

Although a considerable number of academic articles and chapters have been written on the subcomponents of political crime, only a handful of English-language books (sole-authored or edited) have been published on the general subject, including Proal's *Political Crime* (1898/1973); Schafer's *The Political Criminal* (1974); Roebuck and Weeber's *Political Crime in the United States* (1978); Ingraham's *Political Crime in Europe* (1979); Turk's *Political Criminality* (1982a); Kittrie and Wedlock's *The Tree of Liberty* (1986); Tunnell's *Political Crime in Contemporary America* (1993b); Hagan's *Political Crime* (1997); and Kittrie's *Rebels With a Cause* (2000). This literature has contributed to our understanding of the role of politics in the creation of and response to criminal acts.

Some of the early literature suffered from problems that were inevitable, however, since it was produced when few studies on the subject had been published. These difficulties, listed in increasing importance, include the following:

1. The analysis is ahistorical; there is little appreciation of the long-standing difficulty with political crime.

2. They ask more questions than they answer.

3. They are overly pretentious, polemical, or philosophical.

4. They are conservative in tone.

5. The examples marshaled are confined mainly to a discussion of political crime in western democracies.

6. The literature is dated.

7. The research is highly anecdotal or focuses primarily on the description of specific cases.

8. They are primarily collections of government or nongovernmental organization reports.

9. Theoretical explanations of causes are overly simplistic or questionable.

10. The types of political crime are not integrated.

11. Few implications for policy are drawn from these studies.

12. Their explanations of the effects of political crime are limited.

13. They focus primarily on anti-systemic political crimes.

14. There is little appreciation of the interconnectedness of causes and effects.

In other words, analysts primarily marshal a static perspective.

This early work on political crime reflected the embryonic state of the field, though some of these problems were still present in most of the literature of the 1970s and 1980s. It is not my goal to correct all of these difficulties—only the most important—but to contribute in some way to the knowledge base.

This book, focusing solely on advanced industrialized democracies during the contemporary period (1960-present)[9]—in particular the three dominant Anglo American democracies: the United States, Canada, and Great Britain— explains the nature and dynamics of political crime. These countries are in stark contrast to lesser-developed states that may have an authoritarian or totalitarian government and economies based primarily on agricultural and/or raw materials production. Most state agencies in advanced industrialized countries are subject to a variety of controls. When intolerable levels of state crime come to public attention, there is often public and governmental indignation, scandal (Markovitz & Silverstein, 1988), or a crisis of legitimacy (Habermas, 1975). Unlike the totalitarian and authoritarian states, Anglo American countries facilitate the expression of citizen discontent and publicize inquiries into political crimes.

The past four decades have been selected because during that time, perhaps more than ever, elaborate controls were established and the legitimacy of state actions was called into question. During the 1970s and 1980s, all of these countries were affected by "belt-tightening" policies and practices situationally referred to as Reaganism, Mulronyism, or Thatcherism (Ratner & McMullen, 1983). This led to a decline in the provision of social services and, in many cases, an increase in public security functions. This situation created the conditions for a variety of injustices, including state crimes. In addition, Canada and the United States are the world's largest trading partners, and their economies are intimately tied through such arrangements as the North American Free Trade Agreement (NAFTA). Finally, this time period also corresponds to what some analysts (e.g., Ingelhart, 1977) call the post-industrial era, one of the most significant historical changes in recent time.[10]

The book builds on the strengths of previous research and analysis, and is interdisciplinary in scope. In general, all evidence is garnered from open source literature, including scholarly and "popular" books and articles and newspaper stories written during this time period. Periodically I conducted interviews with individuals, whom I call my sources, as a part of their job was responsibility for prosecuting or defending so-called political criminals.

Equally important are the types or subtypes of political crime. Each chapter in the book focuses on a dominant variant of political crime. The most important subtypes of political crime are reviewed, including but not limited to, corruption, illegal domestic surveillance, human rights violations, and state-corporate crime.

In addition, a discussion of genocide best rests with totalitarian and authoritarian states, which this book does not focus on. Moreover, a literature review was determined to be redundant; the subject of sabotage is tangential; state crimes of commission and omission are dealt with in the general chapter on state crime; torture is covered in a chapter on state violence; and war crimes are not covered because of the infrequent reliance on these types of charges during the contemporary period in the United States, Canada, and Great Britain. The concluding chapter attempts to deal with the dialectical strategies for dealing with political crime.

SUMMARY

The previous discussion briefly introduced a definition of political crime and its various types, and sensitized readers to the dynamics of political illegalities. The following chapter reviews theoretical explanations of political crime and clarifies how this phenomenon is the product of individuals, situations, organizations, and resource adequacy (which I later call by the acronym the ISOR). The remainder of this book discusses each type of political crime with special attention to its definition, types, history, conceptual issues, typologies, how widespread the problem is, and causes and effects, along with the marshaling of a variety of examples to demonstrate the processes.

The next section of the book focuses on oppositional political crimes. Five major crimes against the state have been recognized in criminal law: subversion, sedition, treason, espionage, and terrorism.

In the following part, five state political crimes—political corruption, illegal domestic surveillance, human rights violations, state violence, and state-corporate crime—are examined. After demonstrating the weaknesses of our current system for dealing with political crime, the conclusion outlines the difficulties in articulating appropriate measures for controlling it.

The Dynamics of Political Crime is an encompassing treatment of the general subject of political crime. This conceptualization goes beyond traditional ones by including activities resulting in social harm, moral transgressions, and civil and human rights violations. This broader definition includes activities that until now were excluded from most studies of political crime.

NOTES

1. Scheingold (1998) continues this tradition. He labels this political criminology. Unfortunately, I believe this unnecessarily confuses traditional political crime with the political ramifications of crime policy.

2. I have used the terms *political crimes, offenses,* and *illegalities* interchangeably throughout this book.

3. Some, but not all, political crimes can be identified as crimes against the social or public order. Violations of this nature "disturb or invade society's peace and tranquility" (Schmalleger, 2002, p. 431).

4. While *state* means a governmental entity, *nation* typically means a group that shares the same language, history, and customs. Thus, it is technically a mistake to confuse a nation with a state or even a country.

5. These alternative definitions began mostly with the scholarship of Sutherland (1949a, 1949b), who encouraged a definition resting on socially injurious behavior. Then, some two and a half decades later, Schwendinger and Schwendinger (1970) expanded the scope of crime by calling for a definition resting squarely on human rights violations. For them, a criminal was an individual, organization, state, or social relationship that denied individuals the right to realize their human potential (see also Bohm, 1993). Racism, sexism, and economic exploitation resulting from profit-maximizing social relations also have been treated as crimes for they violate individuals' basic human rights (e.g., Quinney, 1977). Most recently, Bohm (1993) has suggested a much more inclusive definition of crime, focusing on human rights violations conducted by the state, which are considered political crimes.

6. Although there are a number of books on the past two decades, both Flexner and Flexner (2000) and Joseph (1994) are helpful.

7. And, for whatever reasons, are willing to participate in the "political process" of the very states that these forces seek to alter.

8. One of the problems with political corruption is whether it is a political crime and whether it is a crime against the state or a crime by the state against its citizens. See Chapter 7 for a detailed discussion.

9. It is argued that access to data is easiest in advanced industrialized democracies; thus the findings are more accurate.

10. The post-industrial era includes a shifting in the dominant bases of the economy from manufacturing to the provision of services. There is also an attendant change in issues that concern the public, particularly a movement from material concerns to those of quality of life.

TEST QUESTIONS

Multiple-Choice

1. What type of violent political crime has been most popularly studied since the 1970s?
   a. assassination
   b. internal war
   c. revolution
   d. state violence
   e. terrorism

2. Who distinguished between those acts committed against the government as "political crimes," and those acts perpetrated by the government or state as "political policing"?
   a. Hagan
   b. Ross
   c. Schafer
   d. Sutherland
   e. Turk

3. Contemporary criminologists recognize that crime can be defined as:
   a. an act of deviance
   b. violation of a criminal law
   c. civil or human rights violation
   d. social harm
   e. all of the above

4. What refers to situations where crimes are committed on behalf of, or for, a collection of individuals who are part of a particular group or unit?
   a. occupational
   b. individual
   c. domestic political crime
   d. context
   e. organizational

5. Which of the following is not a political crime?
   a. political assassination
   b. treason
   c. sedition
   d. embezzlement
   e. spying

6. In the field of criminology, to what extent do introductory texts have a section on political crime?
   a. none
   b. some
   c. half
   d. most
   e. all

7. Who developed a relatively acceptable definition of political crime?
   a. Bierne and Messerschmidt
   b. Don and Mike
   c. Turk and Gurr
   d. Ross and Richards
   e. none has been developed

Short Answer

1. What things have changed over the past 20 to 25 years that may have a bearing on any explanation of political crime?

2. What is the difference between a nation and a state?

3. What is the difference between oppositional and state crime?

4. List five Anglo American democracies.

TWO

THEORETICAL EXPLANATIONS
OF POLITICAL CRIME

———•◦•———

Theories are developed and designed to explain the causes and effects of processes and phenomena and to predict likely outcomes. Social science theories and those that cover the subject matter of criminology and criminal justice are no different in this regard. Needless to say, not all theories are appropriate. Often there is a quest to create the "best" theory. Students, scholars, and practitioners should bear in mind that theories should not be judged on whether they are "good" or "bad," but rather on their utility.

Moreover, there are five basic qualities of a useful theory: that it is testable, is logically sound, is communicable, is general, and is parsimonious (Manheim & Rich, 1986, pp. 19-20). To determine this utility, theories (more appropriately, their hypothesis) can be tested, translated into policies or practices, reified, or abandoned (and not necessarily in that order). This process may provide scholars with a certain degree of contentment or complacency by reassuring them that theories are important. It may also be a welcome distraction from other more pressing problems. In order to understand better the dynamics of political crime, I briefly review more general theories of crime and those that are particularly relevant to political illegalities. I then sketch the outlines of a preliminary framework for a revised theory.

IS IT NECESSARY TO HAVE
A THEORY OF POLITICAL CRIME?

Roughly two dominant reasons concern the necessity of a theory of political crime. Those in favor argue that if political crime is ever to be understood, controlled, or eliminated, we need to have a sophisticated explanation. In order to control this type of crime we need to understand why it happens and especially who participates in this type of offense. Once these two components are determined we can propose some general causal principles and then develop and implement better polices and practices designed to control political crime. If responding to political crime is successful (however defined), then we can restore trust in the government and minimize undemocratic sentiments in the population.

By extension, some may argue, if no theory exists, then people may become cynical, lose faith in their representatives and experts, the democratic political process could collapse, and as a result the state would deteriorate.

On the other hand, others may suggest that although a theory of political crime is not necessary, it would be helpful in understanding political crime. Developing a theory is no guarantee of a peaceful existence or coexistence, or of the resolution of conflict, but it allows us to focus our resources better on what needs them most. Doubters may argue, for example, that neither scholars nor the general public needs a theory in order to properly identify the actions of someone like Colonel Oliver North in the Iran-Contra debacle as questionable.

A major problem is that political crime can be located at all levels of government and spread throughout most organizations within the state. In order to fight or reduce political crime, society may benefit from a theory that explains why or how the crimes are committed. Once the point of origin is found, reformers may take steps to resolve the problem, restore accountability, and provide for good government. Since the types of political crimes are very broad, however, perhaps there have to be several theories dealing with the different manifestations of political offenses. In other words, and in all likelihood, there cannot be a general catchall theory to explain political crime.

THEORIES OF POLITICAL CRIME

No generally accepted causal theories of crime, including political crime, exist. Though this hinders our ability to specify an appropriate explanation

---

BOX 2.1 Robert King Merton (1910-)

Merton was born on July 5, 1910, in Philadelphia, Pennsylvania. He received his Ph.D. in Sociology from Harvard University in 1932. His last teaching position was as Professor of Sociology at Columbia University. Merton was designated as a distinguished or special lecturer to numerous universities, institutes, and organizations in the United States and overseas. During his career he was also a member of several important delegations and committees. He is the author of numerous publications, including *Social Theory and Social Structure: Toward the Codification of Theory and Research* (1949); *On Theoretical Sociology: Five Essays, Old and New* (1967); *The Sociology of Science: Theoretical and Empirical Investigations* (1973); and *Contemporary Social Problems: An Introduction to the Sociology of Deviant Behavior and Social Disorganization* (1961) with Robert A. Nisbet. Merton's work has been translated into numerous languages. (Source: Literature Resource Center).

---

for political offenses, we can talk about relevant theories. Few scholars have developed a theory of political crime. Merton (1938, 1964, 1966) provided one of the earliest explanations that, in part, touches on political crime. According to his anomic theory of deviance (i.e., strain theory), individuals live in a society that has a considerable amount of "structural/dysfunctionalism." This, in turn, leads people to experience an ends/means discrepancy. These processes combined together create stress. In order to minimize the discomfort, individuals have five options, one of which is rebellion (nominally a type of political crime). Merton's anomic theory of deviance, which partially explains political illegalities, is used by Kelly (1972) and Alexander (1992a, 1992b). Unfortunately, Merton's theory, regardless of who uses it, is too limited an explanation for a more encompassing understanding of political crime.

Similarly, Morn (1974) suggests that "sequential stages . . . in successive combination might account for the development of a political criminal" (p. 73). The first are what he calls "predisposing conditions or background factors, the conjunction of which forms a pool of potential political criminals. These conditions exist prior to an individual's decision to commit a political

---

BOX 2.2   Austin T. Turk (1934-   )

Born in 1934 in Gainesville, Georgia, Austin T. Turk is a Professor of
Sociology at the University of California, Riverside. His research and
writing focus primarily on relationships among law, power, inequality,
and social conflict. Major publications include *Criminality and Legal
Order* (1969), *Legal Sanctioning and Social Control* (1972), and *Political
Criminality: The Defiance and Defense of Authority* (1982). Turk is a
Fellow and former President of the American Society of Criminology. He
has been a Trustee of the Law and Society Association, as well as Chair
of the American Sociological Association's Section on Crime, Law and
Deviance. His most recent publications include three entries in the
Encyclopedia of Crime and Justice (2002): "Assassination," "Terrorism,"
and "Crime Causation: Political Theories."

---

crime and by themselves do not account for his behavior." Some of the
conditions include the concept of strain and "a political problem solving
perspective." The latter consists of "situational contingencies which lead to
the commission of political crimes by predisposed individuals" (Morn, 1974,
pp. 73-74). Morn creates a five-stage "developmental model" consisting of
(1) strain, (2) "political problem solving perspective," (3) some sort of turning point, (4) commitment to act, and (5) engaging in the political crime.
Although he recognizes many of the limitations of his idea, the cases from
which he builds his model may be too ideographic to form the generaliza-
tions he did.

An alternative perspective has been offered by Turk (1982a). His structural conflict theory posits that although power and inequality are important
factors in explaining political crime, the cultural gap between offenders and
authorities is what establishes this divide. Turk's theory is interesting, but it
is limited in its explanatory power. Merton's, Morn's, and Turk's theories are
useful in describing, and in some cases explaining, various types of political
crime, but they are not very helpful in accounting for all the vagaries of this
phenomenon. What needs to be understood is political crime's dynamic
nature, and linking macro- with micro-level processes in political crime
(e.g., Frenkel-Brunswik, 1952).

THE BROADER CONTEXT

Research on political crime has often taken either a static perspective or maintained that political crime results primarily from either state or oppositional activities. Like so many other phenomena in the social and natural sciences, the process of political crime follows an interactive, iterative—or what I call "dynamic"—pattern. In short, building on Newtonian physics and political conflict research (e.g., Holsti, Brody, & North, 1981; Lichbach, 1987), nothing in nature is static and neither is political crime. One of the central hypotheses underlying the bulk of this book is that political crime results from the interaction between anti-systemic crime and state crime.

In an effort to illustrate how dynamic political crime can be, we can look at an example of a pattern whereby state crimes can cause oppositional crimes and vice versa (e.g., Balbus, 1977). For instance, the history of the country of Israel is replete with periods of Israeli state terrorism (as well as anti-Arab–settler violence) that motivated Palestinian anti-systemic terrorism, which in turn caused Israeli security responses against the Palestinian people and "terrorist organizations" (Chomsky, 1983; Miller, 2000). When this dynamic is recognized, blame can be directed against all participants in a conflict (e.g., individuals, organizations, and countries), not simply against one party. This is not to say that oppositional political crime leading to state crime and vice versa is a sufficient explanation to understand this phenomenon, but it is a reasonable hypothesis.

Political crime does not exist in a vacuum. Rather, as previously mentioned, it is affected by a series of factors that are endemic to the people who commit the crimes, the occupations these people hold, the organizations that employ them (or that they are members of), and more generally the context in which a particular crime exists. Because political crime is affected by an individual's state of mind, we need to turn to psychological theories. Political crime is also contingent upon cultural, economic, organizational, political, and social influences, usually collectively referred to as social structure. Thus, political crime is a response to a variety of subtle, ongoing, interacting, and changing psychological and structural factors manifested by perpetrators, victims, state agencies, and audiences.[1]

A vast array of theories may shed light on political crime. The first type of theory is "macro" because the theories explain how environmental factors (including institutions, economics, political systems, and culture) affect individuals and groups. Conversely, the latter type is "micro" because the theories explain phenomena pertinent to people, their differences, their mental states, and their interactions.

Linking macro and micro theoretical explanations helps to make sense of political crimes. Relying on these theories forces us to appreciate the actions of specific individuals in tandem with the environment in which they live and work.

Although each of these broad paradigms subsumes several theories, a sub-type of each category may prove to be more useful and have wide currency among several criminologists as explanations of political crime. In the area of structural theory, the social conflict approach has utility. On the other hand, differential association is an appropriate category of psychological theory (Sutherland, 1947).

The most dominant cause behind an act of political crime (oppositional or state) is the desire for power; in particular, gaining, maintaining, or expanding it for an individual and/or his or her organization. Thus, ultimately and in the end, the study of political crime is the study of anarchist criminology (Ferrell, 1998).

In general, structural theories posit that the causes of terrorism can be found in the environment and/or the political, cultural, social, and economic structure of societies. Social-psychological theories specify and explain group dynamics, why individuals join organizations, and how participants (perpetrators, victims, and audiences) affect the commission of acts. Finally, rational choice theories explain participation in organizations and the choice of actions as a result of participants' cost-benefit cognitive calculations.

Psychological Theory

Psychological theories are rooted in individual-level processes. Differential association theory (e.g., Sutherland, 1947) fits conveniently into this paradigm.[2] Sutherland's theory was first used to explain the process by which adolescent males become deviant and engage in delinquent behavior, including joining gangs. Later he reformulated and expanded his theory to include the actions of the wealthy, which he labeled white-collar criminals (Sutherland, 1949a, 1949b). His theory, by logical extension, is applicable to political crime and criminals.

Differential association theory purports that crime is learned behavior that one adopts through affiliating and interacting with others. Favorable attitudes as well as logistical information about how to commit crimes are learned from close friends or acquaintances. In addition, one is socialized into having favorable definitions or attitudes about crime. This latter process is pertinent to understanding how individuals come to regard crime as a viable course of action.[3]

In particular, Sutherland argued that criminal behavior is learned in a process of symbolic interaction with others, primarily in groups.[4] Although nine statements constitute the theory, it is the sixth that Sutherland claimed was *the* principle of differential association. It argues that a person commits crimes because he or she learned more "definitions" (rationalizations and attitudes) that were favorable to violation of the law than definitions that presented lawbreaking as negative (Akers, 1994, p. 93).

Sutherland does not simply claim that associations with "bad company" lead to criminality. Rather, he implies that one learns criminal actions in intimate communication with criminal and noncriminal "patterns" and "definitions." Criminal behavior is explained by one's exposure to others' favorable definitions of crime that are weighed against one's contact with conforming, noncriminal definitions. The process varies according to the "modalities" of association: "That is, if persons are exposed first, more frequently, for a longer time, and with greater intensity to law-violating definitions than to law-abiding definitions, then they are more likely to deviate from the law" (Akers, 1994, p. 93).

Sutherland's theory is as pertinent to political crime and criminals as it is to juvenile delinquency and the vagaries of white-collar crime. It follows that political criminals acquire their behaviors through interactive learning with others. Although there will always be "lone wolves," most political offenders develop a belief (or definitions) that crime offers positive outcomes when the number of definitions favorable to violation of law exceed definitions unfavorable to committing crimes. Whether considering oppositional terrorism by nationalist-separatists or human rights abuses by military officers, it is logical to assume that these behaviors are learned and conducted by individuals within various networks where a system of shared norms and values exists.

Sutherland's theory is able to explain these people's actions as learned within an environment that formally and informally instructs them that criminal behavior (or at least these types of political actions) are favorable, indeed more desirable than actions that do not violate the law. Thus, systematic violations of citizens' rights sanctioned by an organizational program within MI-5 (one of the British National Security agencies) or the Federal Bureau of Investigation (FBI; the American agency for domestic terrorism and other criminal offences of a national matter), for example, can in part be explained by this micro-theoretical perspective.

It follows that Sutherland's theory is able to explain the process by which otherwise law-abiding police officers, acting within their bureaucracy, can violate both the law and individuals' human rights, knowing all the while that their actions are illegal and should be kept secret (see Chapters 6 and 7).

Structural Theory

Structural theories explain human behavior by focusing on the social structures that individuals must function within and on the organizational dictates that affect varieties of behavior. Despite their diversity, these theories share a main concern in that they explain societal organization and the ways that people are affected by institutions, culture, economies, and conflict.

Although several structural theories may be relevant to a discussion of political crime, many scholars regard conflict theory as the most valuable or useful explanation. To make matters more complicated, there are a variety of different conflict theories. They range from conservative to radical perspectives, but they all agree that conflict is a naturally occurring social phenomenon. Special attention should be given to the variety of radical and critical theories, including, but not limited to, Marxist, neo-Marxist, and conflict approaches (Ross, 1998a). Radical conflict theory, some theorists suggest, explains the roots of much political crime that is situated in and emanates from social, political, and economic processes (Roebuck & Weeber, 1978, p. 7). Where conflict theories differ is on its origin, its persistence, its ability to create change, and how it contributes to criminal behavior.

Granted, many theories that have emanated from the radical/conflict tradition are parsimonious, have considerable explanatory power over other efforts, and are widely accepted among many criminologists, as evidenced by their inclusion in a large body of literature in political, white-collar, and state crime research (Ross, 1998a). However, there is considerable discomfort with their ability to be applied to practical policy concerns.

Radical conflict theory traces its origins to the work of Karl Marx. He (along with Frederick Engels) suggested that conflict in society is a result of a scarcity of resources (i.e., property, wealth, power, and jobs). This creates inequalities among individuals and constituencies that in turn lead to a struggle between those who possess these resources and those who do not (Marx & Engels, 1848, p. 9). During the 1960s, almost 150 years after the first articulation of Marx's theories, a number of theorists applied them to crime. These neo-Marxists or "radical" conflict theorists (e.g., Quinney, 1974, 1977) suggested that class struggle affects crime in at least three ways.[5]

Quinney, the leading radical conflict theorist, argued that all crime in capitalist societies (which are fundamentally individualistic and competitive) is considered a manifestation of class struggle whereby people want wealth, power, money, status, and property. In countries dominated by a capitalist mode of production, a culture of competition arises. This is seen as normal and desirable and takes many forms, including criminality, evidenced in poor young men burglarizing residences, corporate executives overcharging consumers, and oppositional terrorist organizations bombing buildings with the hope of effecting social and political change (Quinney, 1977, pp. 53-54; see also Bohm, 1982, p. 570).

Traditional neo-Marxists can be criticized for the disproportionate emphasis they place on "dynamite" as a catalyst of change. The working class and the poor rarely participate in the political process (Gaventa, 1980; Lukes, 1974). Furthermore, the types of activities that are legislated as criminal and that are responded to by the crime control industry are often those behaviors most often engaged in by the poor and powerless.

In order to improve upon explanations that currently exist, I developed a database of people identified by others as political criminals. I collected simple biographical details that would help me understand their motivations for engaging in political crimes. I acknowledge that it is not comprehensive, but use it as a guide to sketch out a new explanation of political crime causation. I also recognize that with additional resources, a more comprehensive picture and even theory could be obtained.

A NEW AND IMPROVED EXPLANATION

Clearly, if the previous discussion has been instructive, a number of theories are more relevant (and useful) than others in explaining political crime in general and the different types in particular. In sum, political crime is the result

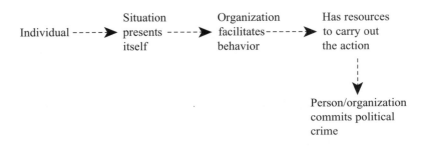

Figure 2.1   The Individual-Situation-Organizational Facilitation-Resource
Adequacy Explanation of Political Crime

of a complex interplay among individuals, situations/opportunities, organizations, and resource adequacy. More important to the understanding of political
crime, however, is what I call the ISOR relationship (ISOR; see Figure 2.1).

Individuals Who Commit Political Crimes

Some people are more predisposed to break the rules than others. Often
called nonconformists or malcontents, they have difficulty with sustained
relationships (especially ones that involve issues of power and authority) in
organizations/institutions, whether a marriage, school, or corporation. In short,
they don't like being told what to do and when to do it. But individuals on their
own don't lead people to take up arms or to break the laws that their organizations are established to enforce. In this respect, the situational theories
may shed light on our endeavor. Typically, however, the situational theories
have focused on crime prevention and opportunity structures (Clarke, 1992).
Clearly, opportunities also present themselves to individuals and organizations.

Situation Presents Itself

On a daily basis, many people and organizations are presented with situations and opportunities that they may take advantage of. At the same time,
these entities are frustrated in their attempts to achieve certain goals. They can
play by the rules (conform to generally accepted norms, including abiding by
the law), or they can selectively or randomly break them.

Organization Facilitates Illegal/Deviant Behavior

Collectivities, also known as organizations, groups, and so on, whether we are talking about terrorist groups or national security agencies, may have as their primary mission the desire to overthrow the government or the quashing of dissent, respectively. The organization may be structured so it provides incentives, or it may simply not have good controls over its members' behavior. Although there is something called bounded rationality (Simon, 1982), individuals, consciously or unconsciously, make cost-benefit calculations about whether they will uphold the law or break it.

Individuals/Organizations Have Necessary Resources

Organizations need the ability and capacity to mobilize resources (i.e., money, personnel, training) in order to accomplish their goals. The argument may arise, like in an untrained army equipped with the most modern equipment, that although they have the resources (e.g., weapons), they may not be able to mobilize properly (e.g., Tilly, 1978). States have a variety of resources, including information control, threat, coercion, infrastructure, organization, and experience.

Whether the political crime is committed by government officials in the name of the state, individual bureaucrats acting for their own personal gain (self-interest), or people and groups desiring to change political and economic systems, it is an example of the mobilization of available organizational or situational resources (e.g., power).

In many respects, this theory is similar to Tilly's (1978) resource mobilization argument, but it differs in the following areas. Tilly suggested that the reason why groups rebel is not because of a relative deprivation, manifested through a process of frustration aggression (e.g., Gurr, 1970). He suggested that it is a combination of circumstances that include timing.

Anti-government groups may demand better housing, jobs, wealth redistribution, social support programs, and universal medical care. They may attempt to organize, protest, march, and strike, each of which is nominally legal in advanced industrial democracies and, in fact, is considered democratic participation. But such activities are often met with resistance from the state and its coercive agencies.

Just as important are the illegalities that the state and its agents commit when segments of the population appear threatening to the political status quo (Turk, 1982a, chap. 4). Wiretapping, illegal surveillance, opening of mail, harassment, intimidation, and even overt force have all been used by states to contain the rising tide of democratic participation.

SUMMARY

Although many political crimes are committed by groups that are formally or loosely structured, whether the groups are oppositional or state organizations, their activities are, in the final analysis, committed by individuals. These people are working within the structural confines of informal or complex organizations, political systems, political economies, and different cultures. They make decisions and act, while often denying that any wrongdoing has occurred.

In general, government response to political crime ranges from apathy to policy advocacy or organizational or political change.[6] In the main, anti-systemic political illegalities are met with resistance or change by states, whereas state crimes are met with apathy, resistance, or demand for change from the public or its elected representatives. Apathy and resistance are the most disconcerting responses to state crime because they prevent its control and future inhibition. For example, a state that is the victim of espionage can simply ignore that a threat to national security has taken place. Alternatively, it can analyze the event or can engage in counterespionage. The ISOR relationship is not simply a resource mobilization theory or a theory of crime prevention through environmental design. Although it has the advantage of breaking up behavior into an easily understandable process, not all outcomes are explained.

Even though conflict and differential association theories were originally developed for understanding nonpolitical crime, they can easily explain political lawbreaking and, as a result, help us to understand the dynamics of political crime. Conflict in general, rather than that motivated by economic factors alone, is the most important reason why people engage in political crime. Groups and in-group socialization are equally important and powerful motivators.

This point is accepted along with the observation that each type of political crime may have a different cause. The relative cause of a particular political offense therefore depends on the situational dynamics.

This chapter has provided a backdrop to an applicable theory of political crime. One must recognize that although creating a theory of political crime may be difficult, it is a necessary though not sufficient step in the process of understanding this phenomenon and establishing better controls or methods of prevention. The following sections are not tests but descriptions and analyses of the most dominant political crimes in contemporary advanced capitalist societies. The next chapter starts with an analysis of oppositional political crimes, which have attracted the lion's share of public, governmental, and academic attention.

NOTES

1. Depending on the circumstances, any of these actors can be an audience.

2. In particular, Burgess and Akers (1968) explicated the rich meanings and relevance of differential association by extending it through a synthesis with learning and behavior modification theories.

3. After some revision, differential association theory was detailed by Sutherland in nine points or statements, all of which are important for understanding the process by which one learns favorable attitudes for doing crime (Sutherland, 1947, pp. 6-7).

4. Many political crimes (e.g., espionage, treason, sedition, terrorism) are committed by individuals without any group support.

5. For a relatively recent treatment of radical/conflict theory, particularly its application to criminology and criminal justice, see, for example, Ross (1998a).

6. See Ross (2000b, chap. 2), for a similar explanation of police response to violence.

TEST QUESTIONS

Multiple-Choice

1. Who argued that criminal behavior is learned in a process of symbolic interactions with others, primarily in groups?
   a. Turk
   b. Sykes
   c. Akers
   d. Proal
   e. Sutherland

2. What theory is Robert Merton most noted for developing?
   a. routine activities theory
   b. learning theory
   c. containment theory
   d. treason
   e. none of the above

3. Which of the following is not true about Sutherland's theory?
   a. crime is a learned behavior
   b. behavior is intrinsic
   c. crime is learned in organizations
   d. applied to political crime
   e. rationalizations for committing crime are learned

4. For a theory to be useful in explaining observations it must meet which of the following standards?
   a. it must be able to be deduced
   b. it must be able to be inclusive
   c. it must be testable
   d. all of the above
   e. none of the above

5. Who developed the five-stage "developmental model" of political crime?
   a. Turk
   b. Morn
   c. Chambliss
   d. Ross
   e. Barak

6. Empirical analysis deals with
   a. how we should use our knowledge
   b. developing and examining values in applying what we've learned
   c. how and what we know
   d. all of the above
   e. none of the above

7. In the ISOR model, what is the most important contributing factor?
   a. the individual
   b. the situation

c. the organization
d. all are important
e. none are important

Short Answers

1. What is the relevance of power to a definition and theory of political crime?

2. Why should we have a theory of political crime?

3. Are there any drawbacks to the ISOR relationship?

4. Who did Sutherland observe in order to develop his theory?

THREE

OPPOSITIONAL POLITICAL CRIMES

———•◦•———

*O**ppositional political crimes* is not simply a term that is found in some dusty old textbook you take off a library shelf, nor did it somehow just magically appear in the public mind. It is part of a larger understanding of crime and serves to organize a variety of diverse actions. Oppositional political crimes are a subset of "crimes against the administration of government" (Schmalleger, 2002, pp. 454-463). This broader rubric includes treason, misprision of treason, rebellion, espionage, sedition, suborning of perjury, false swearing, bribery, contempt, obstruction of justice, resisting arrest, escape, and misconduct in office. Some, but not all, of these crimes have a political motivation. Treason, misprision of treason, criminal syndicalism, rebellion, espionage, sedition, and bribery are traditionally considered to be political crimes, while resisting arrest, bribery, and misconduct in office are not necessarily political offenses.

DELIMITING AND DEFINING POLITICAL CRIME

Although the labels and actions that individuals, organizations, and states have ascribed to anti-systemic political crime differ, this type of action has existed since the birth of the first state. Over the years, the term has been clarified, resulting in a process of including fewer actions. Political offenses have also been defined in a more exacting manner. One of the reasons for this change is that governments, when developing their criminal codes or legislation, look to other countries for examples. Historically, oppositional political offenses have often exacted the most repressive responses from government. Indeed, before the French Revolution

> these crimes were . . . normally requited with the most severe and barbaric punishments, since an attack against the holders of power was . . . an attack on the society itself, comparable to the attack of a foreign country. (Ingraham & Tokoro, 1969, p. 145)

A commonly accepted view is that the lion's share of political crime is anti-government in nature. However, definitions of and the characteristics attributed to political crime have varied considerably over time.[1] Proal (1898/1973), who wrote one of the classic books on political crime, introduced a broad interpretation that included anarchy, assassination, political hatreds, political hypocrisy, political spoliation, the corruption of politicians, electoral corruption, the corruption of law and justice by politics, and the corruption of manners. Many of his terms, however, particularly when interpreted through a 21st century lens, appear ambiguous or irrelevant to contemporary laws.

Today, we might question why Proal chose to identify many of these actions as political crimes. Moreover, due to a variety of factors, since the late 19th century "the doctrine of political crime has become increasingly limited in its scope and application and hedged with exceptions in those European democracies and constitutional monarchies which had adopted it into their codes" (Ingraham & Tokoro, 1969, p. 147). It was not until the 1960s that we had considerable research and writing on the subject of political crime. Schafer (1971, 1974), contrary to the scholars who preceded him, believed that political crime is a type of altruistic behavior motivated by ideological considerations. The actions of political offenders are not entirely selfless, however, as many engage in this activity to satisfy their own needs, too.

Sagarin (1973), in an effort to clarify the meaning and usage of the term, said that a political crime is "any violation of law which is motivated by political aims—by the intent, that is, of bringing about (or preventing) a change in the political system, in the distribution of political power or in the structure of the political-governmental bodies" (p. viii). So, for example, violations of campaign funding laws and civil disobedience might fall under his definition. Although both oppositional and state crimes may be covered by this effort, Sagarin neglects to address the possibility that nonjuridically bound violations, like civil rights abuses, may also be considered political crimes.

BOX 3.1   Stephen Schafer (1911-1976)

Schafer was born on February 15, 1911, in Budapest, Hungary. In 1933 he graduated from Eoetvoes Lorand University with a doctorate in jurisprudence. In the earlier part of his career (1933-1943) he was a practicing attorney in Budapest; later (1947-1951) he was a Professor of Criminal Law at the University of Budapest. He came to the United States in 1961. During the last part of his career he was a professor in the Department of Criminal Justice at Northeastern University (Boston). Among his accomplishments, between 1967 and 1968 he served on the President's National Crime Commission, and in 1969 he worked on the President's Violence Commission. His numerous publications include *Restitution to Victims of Crime* (1960); *The Victim and His Criminal: A Study in Functional Responsibility* (1968); and *The Political Criminal: The Problem of Morality and Crime* (1974). (Source: Literature Resource Center)

Ingraham (1979), in his most classic piece of scholarship, suggests that political crimes are "acts which officials treat as if they were political and criminal regardless of their real nature and the motivation of their perpetrators."

Turk (1984) defines political crime as "whatever is recognized or anticipated by authorities to be resistance threatening the established structure of differential resources and opportunities" (p. 120). Turk (1982a), like Sagarin, does not consider state illegalities legitimate political crimes. He argues that "[n]o matter how heinous such acts may be, calling them political crimes confuses political criminality with political policing or with conventional politics, and therefore obscures the structured relationship between authorities and subjects" (p. 35).

Consequently, he suggests that oppositional political crime should be limited to four types: dissent (e.g., sedition and treason), evasion (e.g., income taxes, draft dodging), disobedience (e.g., civil disobedience), and violence (e.g., terrorism, kidnapping, and assassination). Turk's definition, however, is both under- and overinclusive. He rejects state crimes and mentions a number of actions that, while they may have political overtones, are not political crimes in the strict sense of the term (e.g., income tax evasion and kidnapping).

Table 3.1   Definition Comparison Chart

	Proal (1898)	Sagarin (1973)	Ingraham & Tokoro (1969)	Turk (1982a)
Sedition		x	x	x
Treason	x	x	x	x
Kidnapping		x	x	x
Assassination	x	x		x
Terrorism	x		x	x
Political corruption	x			
Anarchy	x			
Civil disobedience		x		x
Income tax evasion				x
Electoral corruption	x	x		
Political spoliation	x			
Political hatreds	x			
Draft dodging				x
Political hypocrisy	x			
Corruption of manners	x			
Corruption of law and justice by politics	x			

Finally, Hagan (1994, 1997, p. 2) calls any political crime, regardless of the source, "criminal activity committed for ideological purposes." According to this perspective, shoplifting by members of a terrorist group might be equated with sedition by a person opposed to his or her government's policies and practices (see Table 3.1).

TYPOLOGIES

In an effort to improve definitions of political crime and move toward a more analytic perspective, some experts have outlined acts that can and should be subsumed under political crimes. Others have marshaled typologies of political offenses. There is, however, considerable debate over which political offenses in general, and which anti-systemic political crimes in particular, are to be grouped to include in these categories.

BOX 3.2   Barton L. Ingraham (1930-)

Ingraham was born on June 10, 1930, in Paterson, New Jersey. He received his J.D. from Harvard University in 1957, and his Ph.D. in 1972 from the University of California, Berkeley. At an earlier part of his career he was a practicing attorney but later became a professor. Ingraham's last job (1970-1992) was as an Associate Professor at the Institute of Criminal Justice and Criminology, University of Maryland, from which he retired. His publications include *Political Crime in Europe: A Comparative Study of France, Germany, and England* (1979); *The Structure of Criminal Procedure: China, the Soviet Union, France, and the United States* (1987); and (with Thomas P. Mauriello) *Police Investigation Handbook* (1990). (Source: Literary Resource Center)

Packer (1962) subdivided oppositional political crimes into "conduct inimical to the very existence of government, and offenses which affect the orderly and just administration of public business. Treason, . . . sedition or advocacy of overthrow, and espionage are examples of the former," whereas "perjury, bribery and corruption, and criminal libel and contempt by publication" (p. 77) are examples of the latter.

Ingraham and Tokoro (1969), for example, divide political crimes into two types based on intent: pure and mixed/relative ones. Pure political offenses are those behaviors "which, by their very nature, tend to injure the state or its machinery of government either internally, or externally with regard to foreign powers" (p. 196). This delineation includes such crimes as treason and sedition.

Mixed or relative political crimes, on the other hand, include "all criminal acts, regardless of kind, which have as their motive or object some rearrangement of political power within the state and which entail at the same time both an attack on the state and the private interests of citizens" (Ingraham & Tokoro, 1969, p. 146). In other words, acts such as an "assassination of a political figure, robbery, theft or vandalism during an insurrection" would be included in this category.

> **BOX 3.3**   Nicholas N. Kittrie (1928-)
>
> Born on March 26, 1928 (aboard a Polish ship), Kittrie came to the
> United States in 1944 and became a naturalized citizen in 1950. In
> 1950 he received his LLB from the University of Kansas, and his M.A.
> in 1951. He received his LLM in 1963 from Georgetown University
> and his S.J.D. from the same institution in 1968. Currently a Professor
> of Law at American University (Washington, D.C.), Kittrie is also a
> practicing attorney and has been a visiting professor at various univer-
> sities. He is a member of many international committees dealing with
> international and criminal law. His books include *The Right to Be
> Different: Deviance and Enforced Therapy* (1971); *The Tree of Liberty:
> A Documentary History of Rebellion and Political Crime in America*
> (1986/1998, edited with Eldon D. Wedlock, Jr.); *The War Against
> Authority: From the Crisis of Legitimacy to a New Social Contract*
> (1995); and *Rebels With a Cause: The Minds and Morality of Political
> Offenders* (2000). (Source: Literature Resource Center)

In another context, Ingraham (1979) further refines this distinction by making a three-part typology of political crime to include "acts of betrayal," "chal-
lenges to political authority and legitimacy," and "hindrance of official
function." The first refers to behaviors "which deal with the safety and security
of the nation and or society with respect to a foreign enemy." The second
involves "those which concern the safety and security of rulers and the legi-
timizing principles on which their right to rule and their authority depends." And
the last includes "those which involve impediments or embarrassments to rulers
in carrying out functions of government such as foreign relations, taxation,
coinage of money, raising armies, or the administration of law" (pp. 21-23).

Unlike Ingraham, Kittrie (1972) takes a target-based approach and divides
political offenses into five categories including those intended to "weaken or
destroy central political systems" (e.g., treason and sedition); "weaken independent segments or subsystems of the political structure" (e.g., "disruption of
vital industries," etc.); "personal violence and harassment of individual representatives of the political system" (e.g., "capitalists," politicians); "fund raising, designed to underwrite underground political crime phenomena"

Perpetrator	Government	Antigovernment
Violent Crimes	Genocide Police Violence	Assassination Terrorism
Nonviolent Crimes	Corruption Illegal Domestic Surveillance	Sedition Treason Espionage/Spying

Figure 3.1   Typology of Political Crimes

(e.g., robberies); and "activities designed to produce visibility and public support for . . . the protesting political group" (e.g., "disruption of traffic," "unauthorized assembly"). With the exception of "activities designed to weaken or
destroy central political systems" (e.g., treason and sedition), other actions
identified fall under Ingraham and Tokoro's mixed or relative categories,
which are excluded from this treatment of political crime.

One of the most useful typologies divides political crimes into those
behaviors committed by opponents to the regime and actions committed by
those in power or who hold governmental positions (Sagarin, 1973, p. viii; see
also Roebuck & Weeber, 1978). Finally, an equally important typology cutting across these two broad divisions includes two other types of oppositional
political crimes: nonviolent and violent (Beirne & Messerschmidt, 1991,
p. 241); see Figure 3.1.

In sum, typologies of political crime, albeit primarily anti-systemic political offenses, have categorized these actions based on intent, target, degree of
harm done to the state, situational location/profession of the violators, and
degree of violence associated with the crime.

SUMMARY

The previous section outlined seven distinctions advanced up in the scholarly
literature concerning classifications of anti-systemic political crimes.
Nominally, nonviolent political offenses include treason, subversion, sedition,
and espionage. During recent times, however, the majority of oppositional
political crimes and those that have garnered the greatest amount of scholarly,
government, and media attention are violent (e.g., terrorism; see Chapter 5).

In the next chapter I focus on nonviolent political offenses. Although these activities may be mentioned in constitutional or criminal law and a variety of acts, because of their problematic nature and lack of frequency of being prosecuted, the state generally uses other mechanisms to exert some form of social control over so-called political criminals or resisters (Torrance, 1977, 1995).

NOTE

1. An interesting aspect to note is that almost all the individuals who have offered definitions of political crime have been males. This may signal an opportunity for a feminist theory of political crime.

TEST QUESTIONS

Multiple-Choice

1. Who introduced the concept of crimes against the administration of government?
   a. Barak
   b. Proal
   c. Schmallenger
   d. Ross
   e. none of the above

2. Over time, definitions of political crime tend to include
   a. fewer actions
   b. more actions
   c. same number of actions
   d. the number of actions expands and contracts
   e. there is a general tendency to reject political crime

3. In which century were the majority of definitions of political crime made?
   a. 17th
   b. 18th
   c. 19th
   d. 20th
   e. 21st

4. Which of the following is not a category used to define political crime?
    a. intent
    b. target
    c. degree of harm done to the state
    d. ideology of the perpetrator
    e. degree of violence associated with the crime

5. In addition to dividing political crimes into oppositional and state, what is another equally important way to look at them?
    a. violent and nonviolent
    b. internal and external
    c. black and white
    d. all the above
    e. none of the above

6. Which scholar developed one of the first definitions of political crime?
    a. Ingraham
    b. Proal
    c. Ross
    d. Sagarin
    e. Turk

7. In this chapter, how many distinctions are made concerning political crime?
    a. two
    b. three
    c. four
    d. five
    e. seven

Short Answer

1. What is misprision of treason?

2. What is a typology?

3. What is the difference between mixed and relative political crime?

4. From which country does the majority of individuals defining political crime come?

⊰ FOUR ⊱

NONVIOLENT OPPOSITIONAL
POLITICAL CRIMES

———•◦•———

Although law enforcement and national security agencies try to sanction "political" offenders under traditional criminal laws (Kittrie & Wedlock, 1986, p. xi),[1] there are four nonviolent anti-systemic political offenses against the state that in contemporary times have been recognized as crimes by some, but not all, scholars, policymakers, politicians, activists, and jurists. But before examining them it is safe to say that misprision of treason[2] and criminal syndicalism,[3] mentioned in the last chapter, are recognized as oppositional political crimes, but in the last three decades these charges have been rarely applied by courts against political criminal defendants.

In general, subversion, sedition, treason, and espionage are typically included in many of the criminal codes or in legislation governing security and intelligence agencies of advanced industrialized countries.[4] All of these actions have existed since the creation of the first state; however, their codification in legal statutes has varied among countries due to the sophistication of legal codes and the availability of alternative mechanisms for quelling dissent. This chapter defines these offenses and places them in a historical context.[5]

The categorization of what constitutes oppositional political crime varies across Anglo-American democracies. But to put matters in context, most of the laws have their origins in England and were simply integrated by the United States or Canada when these countries were forming their respective criminal codes. Although Great Britain does not have a formal criminal code,

Canada has a federal code and several pieces of relevant legislation. In Canada, for example, the principal groups of oppositional political crimes are "(1) treason, intimidating Parliament, sedition, sabotage, presently found in Part II of the Criminal Code (hereafter Code); and (2) espionage and leakage, currently dealt with in the Official Secrets Act (Canada, 1986a, p. 1). In the United States, on the other hand, while many of the state criminal codes include political offences, at the federal level the Sentencing Commission (October 1987) lists "offences involving national defense," and "treason sabotage, espionage and related offences, evasion of military service, prohibited financial transactions and exporting atomic energy" as typical political crimes. In the United Kingdom many of the oppositional political crimes can be found in the Official Secrets Act, which "covers areas where the state wishes there to be no further threat or debate around certain sensitive security matters."[6] In addition, many of the political crimes are spelled out in anti-terrorism and emergency powers legislation used in connection with the troubles in Northern Ireland.

HISTORICAL PERSPECTIVE

One of the oldest political crimes is treason. In short, treason is "an attempt to overthrow the government of the society of which one is a member" (Schmalleger, 2002, p. 454). In "early common law it was considered 'high treason' to kill the king or to promote a revolt in the kingdom" (Schmalleger, 2002, p. 454). Charging individuals with treason, however, was a convenient way to eliminate those the king or queen (of England) deemed traitors, but more likely the tactic was used to silence real or supposed threats to his or her power. The history of the Tower of London, for example, is embedded with stories of such acts. Those who fell prey to the charge of treason were usually taken to nearby Tower Hill for a public execution and commonly beheaded by an executioner. Once the deed was done, the axman would hold up the head for the assembled crowd to see, then it would be placed on a pole and paraded around the streets of London. Then, in a final act of barbarity, the head and pole would be placed on Tower Bridge (one of a handful of bridges leading into and out of London that cross the River Thames) and crows, ravens, and other birds would strip the head of its flesh. Eventually the skull would fall into the river. It is alleged that almost 1,500 people lost their lives this way (Ackroyd, 2001).

In contemporary time, although treason is mentioned in the U.S. Constitution (Article III) and several federal statutes, the legislation concerning sedition, sabotage, and espionage is embedded in a variety of Congressional acts and other documents (Archer, 1971). Some of these include, for example, the Espionage Act (1917), Sedition Act (1918), Smith Act (1940), McCarran Act (1950),[7] Internal Security Act (1952),[8] and Communist Control Act (1954).[9] Needless to say, "similar, and often even more sweeping, laws (such as those against 'criminal syndicalism') have been enacted by state legislatures and by local governments" (Turk, 1982a, p. 59). Advanced industrialized democracies also have so-called emergency legislation that has political overtones, including provisions that would be considered violations of generally accepted civil liberties during normal times.

Canada, for example, had the War Measures Act (now revised as the War Powers Act) and implemented it during the two world wars and the 1970 "October Crisis" (Corrado & Davies, 2000; Ross, 1995c). Great Britain has relied on a series of special legislation. During World War I and II the British parliament passed the Defence of the Realm (DORA) laws. These allowed the leadership "unlimited power" in its efforts to maintain public safety and national security (Ingraham, 1979, p. 292). "The regulations where not limited to combating external political crime. . . . They regulated virtually any aspect of civilian life which the Government felt was expedient or necessary for public safety or the defence of the nation" including banning "dog shows, the supplying of cocaine to actresses, as well as limiting freedom of the press" (pp. 292-293). Initially the 250 DORA laws were enforced by the military, but when these became too great a drain on resources, "civil magistrate courts" could conduct trials for minor offences and exercise summary jurisdiction (pp. 292-293). In 1939, on the eve of World War II, the British government passed new special legislation called the Emergency Powers (Defense) Act. Although the act was slightly revised in 1940, it was similar in content to the previously instituted DORA laws, but now encompassed 500 laws (Ingraham, 1979, pp. 294-295). This act was eventually terminated after the war.

In England, in 1889, the Official Secrets Act was passed. "This law made it a misdemeanor punishable by imprisonment for up to one year or fine for a person wrongfully to communicate information which he had obtained owing to his position as a civil servant" (Ingraham, 1979, p. 297). In 1911, the act was revised, making it a felony with a possible sentence of 3 to 7 years if an individual "'for any purpose prejudicial to the safety or interests of the State' to approach any military or naval installation or other prohibited place or to make, obtain, or publish or communicate with others information, sketches, or notes which might help an enemy" (p. 298). Also in England, during the past century, two acts had the net effect of controlling anti-government demonstrations by various dissenters: the Incitement to Disaffection Act (1934) and the Public Order Act (1936). Great Britain has also relied on the Prevention of Terrorism Act and has used it frequently in connection with policing its Northern Irish troubles (Ross, 2000a).

In the United States, in the wake of the attacks on the World Trade Center and the Pentagon on September 11, 2001, Congress passed what is commonly referred to as the U.S.A. Patriot Act, which has given both state and federal law enforcement more power in investigating and charging individuals suspected of terrorism. This type of legislation and its attendant procedures is considered by many to be quite controversial. In short, during times of national emergency, by attempting to combat real or imagined threats, the government and its criminogenic agencies may violate basic values of due process and fairness (Mannle & Hirshel, 1988, p. 178).

Moreover,

> diverse mechanisms and criminal or quasi-criminal sanctions for the control of political offenses and the punishment of political offenders likewise have been established. Federal and state laws have relied not only on penal sanctions but also on loyalty oaths, security investigations, the exclusion and expulsion of politically suspect aliens, the calling up of the military, the imposition of martial law, and the confinement of suspect populations in special camps as tools to maintain political order. (Kittrie & Wedlock, 1986, p. xii)

Nevertheless, these crimes represent "the most serious offenses . . . [mainly] because such conduct jeopardizes the security and well-being of the whole nation and its inhabitants . . . these acts are rarely committed and even more rarely charged" (Canada, 1986b, p. 1).

Regardless of where the codification of these offenses is located (penal codes, special legislation, etc.), most informed analysts believe that these crimes threaten the security of the state and its society. Because *security* is an amorphous term and practice (Saltstone, 1991), it makes identification, arrest, and prosecution of individuals committing so-called political crimes variable. This has inspired Turk (1982a) to comment that, "[a]mong the distinguishing features of such laws are their explicit politicality, their exceptional vagueness, and their greater permissiveness with respect to enforcement decisions and activities" (p. 54). Later he adds, "Not only is it inherently difficult to specify the meanings of . . . [many political crimes], it is generally in the interest of authorities to leave themselves as much discretion as possible in dealing with intolerable political opposition" (p. 62).

This situation has stimulated a number of reforms of various countries' criminal codes, especially those sections that deal with political offences.[10] Before reviewing the different anti-systemic political crimes, a discussion of dissent (which is relevant and easily and typically confused with oppositional political crimes) is provided as a necessary backdrop.

DISSENT

The simplest definition of *dissent* is a "difference of opinion." In the context of political crime, dissent is an "ideological label" given

> by national security agencies or those assuming this mandate to social conducts and/or opinion held by citizens of diverging political learning. It follows . . . that dissent cannot be recognized by a determined behavior of social actors, but rather by the limits (of either an ethical or a formal nature) set to what is considered acceptable social and political behavior. (Faucher & Fitzgibbons, 1989, p. 139)

Further complicating matters is the fact that dissent, and the behaviors it refers to, are embedded with other political crime concepts and practices. According to Turk (1982a),

> [d]issent includes any mode of speaking out against the personages, actions, or structures of authority. . . . Each form of resistance may vary in regard to whether it is calculated or spontaneous (or instrumental versus expressive) and organized. (p. 100)

Regardless, dissent is

> characteristically a higher-class form of resistance, particularly insofar as it is an articulate elaboration of a reasoned political philosophy. Grumbling, diffuse complaints, or emotional rhetoric with little if any empirical grounding or

logical coherence are more likely to characterize the "dissent" of those
lower-class persons who do speak out against the given order. (Turk, 1982a,
p. 100)

Almost anyone can express dissent; thus the characteristics of those who
engage in this behavior are numerous. Dissenters include anyone or any group
that proffers an opinion that detracts from the status quo (e.g., media personnel, politicians, clergy, conscientious objectors, social movements; see,
e.g., Hagan, 1997, chap. 4).
   Moreover,

[i]n the absence of a developed political consciousness, or sensitivity, dissent
is likely to be an expression of a more or less vague resentment of one's
political fate rather than an instrumental action intended to achieve any
specific changes in the political environment. (Turk, 1982a, p. 101)

Undoubtedly, both governments and states have flexible criteria for identifying and responding to "acceptable and unacceptable dissent." Franks
(1989) suggests that dissent can be classified into four categories based on the
dimensions of legal-illegal and legitimate-illegitimate (i.e., legal-legitimate,
legal-illegitimate, illegal-legitimate, and illegal-illegitimate). Typically
authorities (law enforcement and national security) accept legal-legitimate dissent but reject illegal-illegitimate dissent. "The other two categories are contentious. From a liberal-democratic viewpoint, a goal of government and
society should be to include as much as possible in the legal-legitimate category" (Franks, 1989, pp. 6-7).
   The legal mechanisms for controlling dissent have been criticized because
they typically "directly sanction or prohibit unwanted behavior by labelling it
illegal. Instead, the law permits authorities to investigate, study, and report.
This results in indirect penalizing" (Franks, 1989, p. 1), or what Whyte and
MacDonald (1989) term "partial sanctioning."
   This includes "hidden penalties such as negative personnel reports, or refusal
to hire. . . . These sorts of activities do not fit within the liberal-democratic legal
tradition. They are outside standard legal and judicial concepts and practices"
(Franks, 1989, p. 1). Whyte and MacDonald (1989) conclude that Western
democracies have lost the ability to use legal concepts in the field of national
security regarding dissent. Consequently, "this leads to extreme problems in
making a distinction between legal and illegal dissent" (Franks, 1989, p. 11).

SABOTAGE

The charge of sabotage is primarily restricted to offenses committed during time of war and refers to "deliberate or underhand damage or destruction, especially carried out for military or political reasons" ("Sabotage," 2002). Alternatively, sabotage can include disruptive actions taken by workers or "the enemy" against a business or factory during wartime or a trade or labor dispute.

Furthermore, sabotage "technically means the willful destruction or injury of, or defective production of, war-material or national-defense material, or harm to war premises or war utilities" (*Black's Law Dictionary*, 1994, p. 1335). There may be some debate over what, exactly, constitutes war and national defense material. According to the United States Code, Title 18 (Crimes and Criminal Procedure), Chapter 105 (Sabotage), Section 2151 (Definitions) "War and national defense material" includes

> arms, armament, ammunition, livestock, forage, forest products and standing timber, stores of clothing, air, water, food, foodstuffs, fuel, supplies, munitions, and all articles, parts or ingredients, intended for, adapted to, or suitable for the use of the United States or any associate nation, in connection with the conduct of war or defense activities.

SUBVERSION

Subversion refers to the act of "overthrow[ing] that which is established or existing" and is a term "used to delegitimize ideas and activities opposed to the established order, and hence to legitimize the states' acting against them, even though those ideas and activities are lawful" (Franks, 1989, p. 10).[11] Building on Franks's (1989, pp. 10-11) typology, the state defines subversion as an action that is "legal but illegitimate. Subversion is defined through a supposed link between internal dissent and so-called deviant foreign influences." In Great Britain, the 1989 Security Service Act defines subversion as "actions intended to overthrow or undermine parliamentary democracy by political, industrial or violent means" (s.1(2)). "This definition clearly includes political and industrial activity that is both peaceful and lawful" (Gill, 1995, p. 91).

During the early part of the 20th century, in many Western democracies, individuals and organizations espousing, advocating, and/or practicing a variety of different political ideologies (e.g., anarchism, bolshevism, communism, fascism, nationalism, Nazism, pacifism, socialism, separatism) were labeled "subversives." These groups were blamed for widespread industrial unrest, including bombings. They were feared by governments, their bureaucracies, and the elite (e.g., Goldstein, 1978).

In both Canada and the United States, for example, the Royal Canadian Mounted Police and the Department of Justice, respectively, formed "Radical" or "Red-hunting" squads. They frequently infiltrated, arrested, and, in some cases, deported alleged, suspected, or self-confessed subversives (Brown & Brown, 1978; Ellis, 1994, pp. 39-59; Sawatsky, 1980).

During the 1960s, in the United States, the term *subversive* was used by authorities and moral entrepreneurs to describe many student protesters; the New Left; and African American, Chicano, and Native American nationalists. These political and social movements led in some cases to spin-off political parties, militias, and terrorist organizations such as the Weatherman (later called Weather People), Black Liberation Army, La Raza, and the Symbionese Liberation Army. In Canada, the *Rasemblement pour Resistance* led to a variety of Québécois nationalist separatist terrorist groups (Ross, 1995c; Ross & Gurr, 1989). And in the United Kingdom (Northern Ireland in particular), during the 1960s, police crackdowns and confrontations with civil rights protestors motivated a number of individuals to rekindle Irish hatred of the British and join or form Irish Republican Army terrorist cells.

In short, because of the subjective nature of interpreting acts of subversion many jurists and observers find the term very contentious (e.g., Spjut, 1974).

SEDITION

Sedition has been defined as the "incitement of resistance to or insurrection against lawful authority" (*Webster's New Collegiate Dictionary,* 1980, p. 1037). In other contexts it is "communication or agreement intended to defame the government or to incite treason" (Schmalleger, 2002, p. 456). In Canada, the Code identifies an individual as guilty of sedition if he or she "teaches or advocates . . . the use, without authority of law, of force as a means to accomplish a governmental change within Canada" (Borovoy, 1985, p. 156). In the United States, the Sedition Act of 1798, ch. 74, 1 Stat. 596, criminalized any scandalous article written about the President or Congress. Later federal law defined seditious conspiracy as, "If two or more persons in any State or Territory, or in any place subject to the jurisdiction of the United

States, conspire to overthrow, put down, or destroy by force the Government of the United States, or to levy war against them, or to oppose by force the authority thereof, or by force to prevent, hinder, or delay the execution of any law of the United States, or by force to seize, take, or possess any property of the United States contrary to the authority thereof" (18 U.S.C., Section 2384).

More commonly, those determined by authorities to have engaged in sedition are charged with "seditious libel" (Thomas, 1972). Thus, the problem is embedded in the larger issue of freedom of speech, especially that which criticizes government (Borovoy, 1985; Foerstel, 1998, chap. 1). Furthermore, the criteria for defining acts as seditious libel are dynamic and subject to changes in political, economic, and social conditions. In its most expansive form, however, seditious libel may be said to embrace any criticism—true or false—of the form, constitution, policies, laws, officers, symbols, or conduct of government (Stone, 1983, p. 1425).

Understandably, the biggest difficulty with the crime of sedition is being able to specify "at what point in the continuum between the thought and the deed is it appropriate for the law to intervene" (Borovoy, 1985, p. 156). In general, "Speech which is likely to result in imminent violence is arguably dangerous enough to warrant legal intervention. On the other hand, speech which is not likely to culminate in this way does not warrant such intervention" (Borovoy, 1985, p. 156).

Sedition laws date back to early English history where the criminalized act was called seditious libel. In short, seditious libel was saying something negative about someone in power (i.e., kings, queens, and/or their ministers). The truth of a statement was not relevant to the charge. A rule of thumb at that time was that jurists believed that the greater the truth, the greater the libel. As a frequent penalty, quite often offenders would have their hands cut off.

The first significant challenge to the sedition laws, at least in America, came in 1735 when John Peter Zenger, a printer, accused the governor of Massachusetts of being a liar and a thief. In contrast to previous rulings, it was determined that the truth was a defense; thus, Zenger was acquitted (Foerstel, 1998, pp. 2-3). In 1918, in an effort to shore up support for the entrance of the United States into World War I, and to prevent criticism of the war, which would damage recruiting efforts, the act was amended, becoming more specific, and was popularly referred to as the Sedition Act. During this time, close to one thousand individuals were incarcerated under state or federal sedition laws because they were against World War I, or because of their "controversial" union activities, or religious and political beliefs (Kohn, 1994). However, it was not until 1971 that the Espionage Act was once again considered to quiet the news media. In that year, Daniel Ellsberg, a scientist working for the RAND Corporation and a consultant to the Department of Defense, released information to the *New York Times* about Pentagon bombing missions in North Vietnam (Herring, 1993). The government tried unsuccessfully to block the publication through the rarely used legal mechanism called prior restraint (Foerstel, 1997).

In the United States, judges and jurists generally use what is called the "clear and present danger test" to determine whether communications are dangerous and/or seditious. In other words, an individual who says something that can be interpreted as a statement that may lead to immediate harm, like shouting the word *fire* in a crowded theater (example given by Justice Oliver Wendell Holmes, Jr., in *Schenck v. United States*, 1919) can be charged and thus does not have protection under the free speech guarantees of the Constitution. The question is whether or not it is appropriate to label the speech seditious or merely an expression of a political position.

Individuals are occasionally charged with seditious conspiracy, but it is difficult for the government to secure a conviction for this type of crime.

> Conspiracy is established by inference from the conduct of the parties. It is very rare that the agreement between the parties can be established by direct evidence; the evidence offered is usually purely circumstantial. To prove the agreement, evidence such as hearsay, which would normally be inadmissible to establish any other criminal offense, may be admitted to show links in a chain of circumstances from which the common agreement may be inferred. (Grosman, 1972, p. 142)[12]

Too often governments have tried to prevent people and opposition groups from expressing dissent by charging them with sedition. Rather than protecting the common good, however, this kind of charge backfires, because it reinforces the perception and perhaps the reality of arbitrary state power. Alternatively, because of the cumbersome nature of the Sedition Act, the government has found it more convenient to charge, frustrate, and in some cases convict individuals and organizations under a number of existing acts. This process virtually places plaintiffs under a gag order. For example, in 1978, *The Progressive,* a left-leaning magazine, was about to publish an article that explained, using readily accessible library resources, how to build a hydrogen bomb. The federal government quickly found out about this, and believing this communication to be harmful to the well-being of the United States (and a violation of the Atomic Energy Act), issued a prior restraint order against the magazine.[13] This legal maneuver prevented the article from being published for 6 months, but it eventually appeared in November 1979. Similarly, former Central Intelligence Agency (CIA) employees who have published "tell all" books (e.g., Agee, 1975; Marchetti & Marks, 1975; Snepp, 1977) about their work for the organization have been sued because they violated a secrecy agreement that they signed when they entered government service, which in most cases required them to vet their material through the agency's prepublication review process.[14]

TREASON

Treason refers to overt (i.e., nonsymbolic) acts aimed at overthrowing one's own government or state or murdering or personally injuring the sovereign (king or queen) or the sovereign's family (Chapin, 1964; Ivey, 1950). In Canada, Section 46 (Subsection 1) of the Code differentiates between high treason and treason. The former crime includes restraining, injuring, killing, or attempting to kill the king or queen; engaging in war against Canada; and assisting an enemy of Canada in time of war or assisting a country that has "hostilities" against Canada (Canada, 1986b, p. 12). The latter is defined by the Code, Section 46, (Subsection 2) as using force or violence against Canada with the purpose of overthrowing it; giving a foreign agent information that would affect the safety or proper defense of Canada; and helping an individual commit treason or high treason (Canada, 1986b, p. 13).

In the United States, the Constitution (Article III, Section 3) states that, "Treason against the United States, shall consist only in levying War against them, or in adhering to their Enemies, giving them Aid and Comfort." Federal statutes use similar language, such as,

> Whoever, owing allegiance to the United States, levy war against them or adheres to their enemies, giving them aid and comfort within the United States or elsewhere is guilty of treason and shall suffer death, or shall be imprisoned not less than five years and fined under this title but not less than ten thousand dollars ($10,000); and shall be incapable of holding any office under the United States. (18 U.S.C., Section 2381)

Many states, in either their legislation or constitutions, also have specific sections that refer to treason (Schmalleger, 2002, p. 455).

Thus, it is

> a criminal offense to publish false, scandalous, and malicious writings against the government, if done with intent to defame, or to excite the hatred of the people, or to stir up sedition or to excite resistance to law, or to aid the hostile designs of any foreign nation against the United States. (Packer, 1962, p. 82)

Given the burden of proof, the appropriateness of the charge of treason is often debatable. Historically, treason has been a slippery concept. Although it is generally recognized as a legitimate criminal offence, it is frequently used by authorities, opinion makers, moral entrepreneurs, and pundits as a label to describe the actions of nonviolent dissenters. Furthermore, few individuals and organizations have been prosecuted for treason.

For example, in the history of the United States fewer than 50 cases involving treason have been prosecuted (Hurst, 1971, p. 156). "[S]ince the adoption of the Constitution there have been few treason prosecutions in United States history (less than forty pressed to trial, even less convictions, and no federal executions" (Ingraham & Tokoro, 1969, p. 148). "The legal history of treason and related offenses in England is similar" (Turk, 1984, p. 121). A review of this record reinforces the perception that some cases clearly represent textbook cases of treason and others do not. Moreover, two items are crucial if the charge of treason is to be applied appropriately: the citizenship of the individuals and the place where the action has taken place.

Because treason is a violation of allegiance, for the charge to have merit, one must be a citizen of the United States or engaged in the process of naturalization. Thus resident aliens are assumed to be on their way to becoming citizens. If, on the other hand, you have lost, renounced, or were never a citizen of the United States (e.g., tourist, visitor, or student), the charge of treason does not apply (Hagan, 1990, p. 444; Schmalleger, 2002, p. 455).

Normally, the offense of treason needs to be committed inside the United States, but jurisdiction has expanded to outside America. Several persons (like Ezra Pound) were prosecuted for their broadcasts in foreign countries during World War II (Packer, 1962, p. 80). One of the most famous cases was against the rather eccentric pro-Fascist American poet-writer Ezra Pound (Cornell, 1969). During World War II the fascists, who were in power in Italy, allowed him to broadcast in English from Rome. Later he was arrested and charged by the U.S. government with treason. During the trial Pound claimed that his actions were patriotic. He was "institutionalized after a questionable trial resulting in a verdict of 'unsound mind' [and] kept in St. Elizabeth's Hospital, Washington D.C. from 1945 to 1958 when upon petition he was released as incurably insane, but not "dangerous'" (Turk, 1982a, p. 53).

ESPIONAGE/SPYING

Spying, also called sub-rosa crime or espionage (the act or practice of spying), is one of the most well-known acts of treason (Bryan, 1943). This type of political crime refers primarily to secretly obtaining information or intelligence about another, and typically hostile country, its military, or weaponry (Bryan, 1943; Laqueur, 1985). In short, espionage occurs when "gathering, transmitting or losing information or secrets related to national defense with the intent or the reasonable belief that such information will be used against the United States" (Schmalleger, 2002, p. 455).

Various types of espionage exist, including "black espionage," a term for such things as "covert agents" involved in classical forms of spying, and "white espionage," referring to "spying via space satellites, through code-breaking, or technical collection" (Hagan, 1990, p. 444).

Espionage has been practiced since early recorded history and is mentioned in classic texts such as the Bible (e.g., when the Israelites surveyed the land of the Canaanites) and Chinese military philosopher and practitioner Sun-Tzu's *Art of War* (Hagan, 1990, p. 444). In 1917, the U.S. Congress passed the Espionage Act (18 U.S.C., Section 2384). Despite minimal attention in the criminological literature, the political crime of espionage "is more costly than traditional crime and has altered post–World War II economic and political history. It was estimated that during the Cold War theft of Western technology by the Soviet Union cost billions in future defense expenditures to counter Soviet improvements" (Hagan, 1990, p. 444). The information that has been revealed not only has had an effect on national security, but it has led to the deaths of double agents.

Numerous reasons exist to explain why individuals, organizations, and states spy. At the level of the individual, some factors include the person's motivation, ideology, potential embarrassment over being compromised, ego, and sexual favors. At the organization or state level, espionage can be part of the broader mission of intelligence gathering and its goal, which is primarily to gain some sort of competitive advantage (Hagan, 1990, p. 444). And recently, a

> major shift [has been detected] in the motivations of spies East and West from the ideological, Cold War fifties to the materialistic/hedonistic eighties and nineties. The ideological motivation has been replaced for the most part by mercenary considerations. (Hagan, 1990, p. 444)

Espionage/spying is conducted by citizens and foreigners alike. We usually hear about it when Americans are arrested for spying on behalf of a foreign country in the United States. Alternatively, foreigners are arrested for espionage inside the United States, and finally there are occasions when Americans are detained and charged with spying in foreign countries. In short, when foreigners are caught doing it, they are usually briefly detained and then deported. When citizens are accused of these types of acts, they are typically incarcerated, and they may even be executed.

One of the most well-known cases of espionage in the United States concerned the activities of Julius and Ethel Rosenberg. In 1950, during the height of the Cold War, they were arrested, tried, convicted, and on June 19, 1953, the Rosenbergs were executed for obtaining classified information on the highly secret atomic bomb for the Soviet Union (Garber & Walkowitz, 1995; Neville, 1995; Wexley, 1977).

In recent years, a number of spying operations both in the United States and abroad have received widespread public attention. One of the most pervasive operations is that of Echelon (Hagen, 1997; Richards & Avey, 2000; Wright, 1998). Although its existence was originally denied by the U.S. National Security Agency, the program apparently monitors or has the capability to track every electronic transmission, including cell phone calls and e-mail messages. It became a scandal in Europe in February 2001 when it was discovered that the CIA was spying on behalf of American businesses (Redden, 2000). Alternatively, since 1986, the FBI has been using Carnivore, which intercepts all e-mail traffic in and outside of the United States. Less serious, but probably more pervasive, are real or purported bugging incidents. For example, in February 2002 it was revealed that the CIA had planted listening devices in the rooms of Japanese officials during the most recent round of trade negotiations between the United States and Japan.

Exhibit Box 4.1   Julius and Ethel Rosenberg

In the 1950s, at the height of Cold War hysteria, Julius and Ethel Rosenberg were arrested and charged with treason: specifically, passing secrets of America's atomic bomb to Soviet agents. It was alleged that this information served as a catalyst for the Soviet/Russian atomic program. It did not help that both Julius and Ethel were, at one time, members of the American Communist Party. They were both sentenced to death and on June 19, 1953, despite their claims to innocence, considerable debate about the quality of the evidence presented at their trial and the impartiality of the judges, a large public protest, a stay of execution, appeals to the Supreme Court and the president of the United States, and the fact that they had two small boys, they were electrocuted at Sing Sing Penitentiary in Ossining, New York.

Despite promises of leniency by the prosecution, the so-called co-conspirators received severe sentences ranging from 3 to 18 years. The Rosenberg case has been the subject of numerous articles and books, both popular and scholarly. Two documentaries have been produced: *The Unquiet Death of Julius and Ethel Rosenberg* (1974), and *Landmark American Trials: Julius and Ethel Rosenberg* (1999).

During the past two decades several FBI and CIA officials and members of the armed services have been arrested, charged, and/or convicted of espionage. Almost always it is because they had sold classified documents outlining details of military weapons, equipment, and capabilities to Soviet or Russian intelligence sources (e.g., the KGB). Many were senior staffers in their agencies and had committed these crimes undetected for decades. In 1985, for example, naval Officer John Walker Jr. was convicted of spying on behalf of the KGB for 18 years (Earley, 1988; Kneece, 1986). In 1994, Aldrich H. Ames, a veteran CIA official (and his wife Rosario) were convicted of espionage. Aldrich was given life in prison, and his wife served 5 years. In 1996, Earl Edwin Pitts, an FBI agent for 13 years, was arrested, and a year later he pleaded guilty to espionage. In 1996, Harold J. Nicholson, a CIA station chief, was arrested; 2 years later he was convicted of espionage (Earley, 1998). In

October 1998, retired Army Intelligence analyst David Shelton was convicted of selling secrets to Moscow.

More recently, in the spring of 2001, Robert P. Hanssen, a senior FBI agent, was accused of having illegally transferred sensitive documents to Soviet and then Russian intelligence agents and their organizations since 1985. Hanssen was in a unique position because of his contacts with the CIA and the State Department. Why and how he managed to evade detection for a decade and a half were matters of grave concern to U.S. intelligence officials (Havill, 2001).

Most of the individuals mentioned above as convicted "spies" were sentenced to long stints in maximum security federal penitentiaries, some of them only narrowly avoiding a possible death penalty. The information they provided to the Soviets/Russians had the unfortunate consequence of leading to the deaths or executions of counter or double agents (i.e., Soviet/Russian citizens who were spies on behalf of the United States).

On the other side of the coin, in February 2001, American student John Edward Tobin, who was also a member of the Army reserve but living in Russia, was arrested by Russian officials on charges that he was spying on behalf of the United States. Also in 2001, a handful of Chinese American scholars (i.e., Li Shaomin, Gao Zhan, and Qin Guangguang) working in the People's Republic of China were arrested and accused of spying. After several months in detention they were ultimately released back to the United States ("China Expels Convicted U.S. 'Spy,'" 2001).

After World War II, in Great Britain a number of British citizens who were working in senior intelligence capacities and acting as spies for the Soviet government were detected. These people included Michael Bettaney, George Blake, Anthony Blunt, Guy Burgess, Donald Maclean, Kim Philby, Anthony Price, and John Vassall (Boyle, 1979; Sutherland, 1980). Their presence "proved that internal security was still deficient, causing new problems between Britain and her allies" (Laqueur, 1985, p. 208). Like the American spies, their activity had been going on for decades.

Also in Britain, the National Security Agency (NSA) and the General Command Headquarters (GCH/Q) illegally undertook massive surveillance of activists, trade unionists, and British businesses through a microwave network set up in the 1960s for such purposes. The extent of the activities of this apparatus first came to light in the mid-1970s when *New Statesman* journalist Duncan Campbell revealed the level and sophistication of Signals Intelligence (SIGNIT), later referred to as the ABC affair (Thurlow, 1994).

In Canada, in September 1945, Igor Gouzenko, a rather low-level Soviet cipher clerk, walked into the *Ottawa Journal* and then the Department of Justice, seeking to exchange information for Canadian citizenship. He told officials that the Soviet Union had been spying on Canada. Shortly after, 39 individuals were arrested in two sweeps, including Fred Rosenberg, a Member of Parliament. This led to the establishment of the Kellock-Taschereau Royal Commission of Inquiry, which determined that a large spy ring existed in Canada for the purpose of obtaining atomic secrets. Approximately half of those arrested were convicted of their charges (Sawatsky, 1984).

Between 1956 and 1979 at least 32 government workers from countries such as Cuba, Czechoslovakia, Hungary, Iraq, the People's Republic of China, Poland, and the Soviet Union were expelled from Canada or their governments informed that they could not return to Canada because they were attempting to illegally obtain military secrets, obtain industrial information, or recruit spies, or were engaging in "unacceptable behavior" (Sawatsky, 1980, appendix A).

Most notably during this time period, in 1967, Bower Featherstone, a mapmaker working for the Canadian government, sold classified naval maps to a Soviet spy. He was charged and convicted under the Official Secrets Act, sentenced to 30 months in prison, and ended up serving 10.

During the 1980s, it seemed like there was an endless stream of foreign individuals and countries that allegedly were spying in Canada, including Americans, Cubans, Koreans, and Israelis. In almost all of the cases the individuals were expelled from Canada.

SUMMARY

Objective study of nonviolent anti-systemic political illegalities is complicated by the subtle nuances in the different definitions, the tendency of the state to downplay the political context of charges, and the use of obscure political crime laws, or by using traditional criminal laws against so-called political offenders (Torrance, 1977, 1995), the proliferation of mass media misinformation, and political propaganda that contributes to public ignorance. Some of the obscure statutes that the state uses include inciting a rebellion, obstructing military operations, and sabotage (Mannle & Hirschel, 1988, p. 170). Conventional criminal laws that governments may use to quell political dissenters include violations of city ordinances, disturbing the peace, resisting arrest, and conspiracy to cross state lines to commit a crime (Mannle & Hirschel, 1988, p. 170). When the political situation appears to be in crisis, not only will governments rely on these kinds of statutes, but they will also hastily develop and pass relatively comprehensive emergency legislation. Alternatively, "Most insurrections have been local affairs and have usually been handled under state treason, sedition or subversive conspiracy statutes or under statutes designed to control riots and public disturbances" (Ingraham & Tokoro, 1969, p. 148). Moreover, in the United States, despite the perception that "illegal forms of political dissent [are viewed] as immoral and dishonorable, as well as impermissible," juries typically hesitate to convict political criminals, the state frequently grants "pardons, amnesties, or suspended sentences" after the conditions that motivated the individual have subsided, and if convicted and sentenced to federal prison, the prisoners are often treated more leniently (Ingraham & Tokoro, 1969, p. 149). Although the widespread harm that can be brought by treason, sedition, and espionage are noted, violent events are more dramatic, gain more media attention, and are often more disturbing. An analysis of these actions is treated in the following chapter.

NOTES

1. For a history of legislation concerning offenses against the state in Canada, see Canada (1986a, 1986b) and for a history of legislation supporting about political crimes against the state in the United States, see, for example, Kittrie and Wedlock (1986).

2. In short, "the concealment or nondisclosure of the known treason of another" (Schmalleger, 2002, p. 455).

3. In sum, "advocating the use of unlawful acts as a means of accomplishing a change in industrial ownership, or to control political change" (Schmalleger, 2002, p. 455).

4. In general, we can divide political crimes into violent and nonviolent types. Admittedly we could probably devote a chapter to each of the nonviolent oppositional political crimes; however, since treason, sedition, and espionage charges are rarely applied in the contemporary period, we do not.

5. Noticeably absent is a discussion of civil disobedience. Despite the political nature of civil disobedience, it is largely ignored by most reviews of political crime.

6. Personal correspondence, Steve Wright, February 2002.

7. Required the registration of all Communists and their organizations that existed in the United States.

8. Also known as the McCarran Walter Act; it provided for the expelling of aliens who were suspected of disloyalty to the United States.

9. For a review of these acts see, for example, Packer (1962). Some of these laws have been struck down as unconstitutional (Turk, 1984).

10. For example, in 1986 the Law Reform Commission of Canada noted a series of problems with offenses against the state and suggested that, "Part II of the *Code* and the *Official Secrets Act* are riddled with defects of both form and content" (Canada, 1986b, p. 25).

11. Another discussion of subversion can be found in Grace and Leys (1989).

12. Seditious conspiracy is found in section 60(3) (4) of the Canadian Criminal Code.

13. Prior restraint enables the government to prevent the printing or broadcasting of material that it believes could be harmful in advance of this determination being made by a court. The constitutionality of this power is hotly debated.

14. Some of the authors have detailed this experience in either the preface to their books or in follow-up memoirs (e.g., Snepp, 1999).

TEST QUESTIONS

Multiple-Choice

1. Which of the following is the oldest type of political crime?
   a. espionage
   b. sedition
   c. tax evasion
   d. subversion
   e. treason

2. In what year were Julius and Ethel Rosenberg put to death?
   a. 1961
   b. 1962
   c. 1963
   d. 1964
   e. 1953

3. When was the first sedition act passed in the United States?
   a. 1917/1918
   b. 1945
   c. 1950
   d. 1492
   e. 1798

4. Which of the following is not considered to be an oppositional political crime?
   a. sedition
   b. escape
   c. espionage
   d. treason
   e. all of the above

5. In the United States, the majority of political crimes on the books have their origins in what kind of law?
   a. Canadian
   b. British
   c. state
   d. biblical
   e. none of the above

6. What legal mechanism was used to prevent the publication of Ellsberg's *Pentagon Papers?*
   a. he was arrested
   b. notes were seized from his psychiatrist
   c. probable cause
   d. printing presses were seized
   e. prior restraint

7. In the United States, where is the most prominent place legislation connected to treason is mentioned?
   a. consumers' bill of rights
   b. Constitution
   c. emergency legislation
   d. Pledge of Allegiance
   e. Bill of Rights

Short Answer

1. What are two dimensions of Franks' typology based on?

2. In times of crisis, governments pass "emergency legislation." Identify two of these laws that have been used in recent times and comment on their advantages and disadvantages.

3. What is the most common way the federal government has sanctioned former employees of the CIA who wrote books critical of the agency?

4. In which state were the Rosenbergs executed?

FIVE

VIOLENT OPPOSITIONAL POLITICAL CRIMES

Terrorism

A lthough the crime of rebellion defined as "deliberate, organized resistance by force and arms, to the laws or operations of the government committed by a subject" exists in federal legislation (Schmalleger, 2002, p. 455), over the past three decades it has been rarely applied to individuals and groups. Likewise, in advanced industrialized democracies, reliance on assassination, "a politically motivated killing in which the victims are selected because of the expected political impact of their dying" (Turk, 1982b, p. 82) has been limited. Here the murder is the work of a person of sound mind and not by a mentally deranged person. The major U.S. political assassinations over the past four decades have been those of John and Robert Kennedy, Martin Luther King Jr., and Malcolm X. Although assassination is part of the arsenal of techniques used by terrorists, "pure assassination" is an attempt to eliminate a person and not necessarily to strike fear into the citizens of a country.

Since the early 1960s, however, anti-systemic political terrorism has generated considerable attention.[1] By far the greatest number of incidents of oppositional political crime in advanced industrialized countries during recent times fell under the rubric of terrorism.[2] Understandably, the meaning of the term has been fervently debated and politicized because it is used as a label that powerful individuals, organizations, and states apply sometimes indiscriminately to perceived and actual enemies (Herman, 1982; Jenkins, 1988). This simplistic thinking has encouraged so-called conspiracy theories of terrorism purporting, for example, that the former Soviet Union and its satellite countries launched an offensive against the West through a well-organized and -financed network of terrorist organizations (e.g., Sterling, 1981). Though cursory evidence pointed to Communist support for a number of national liberation organizations, the charges against the "evil empire" now appear to be exaggerated.

DEFINITIONAL AND CONCEPTUAL ISSUES

Following Schmid's (1983) conceptualization,

> terrorism is a method of combat in which random or symbolic victims . . . become target[s] of violence. . . . Through . . . the use or threat of violence, . . . other members of that group [e.g., class, nation, etc.] are [placed] . . . in a state of chronic fear. . . . The victimization of the target is considered extranormal by most observers, . . . [which] creates an . . . audience beyond the target of terror.
> . . . the purpose of . . . [terrorism] . . . is either to immobilize the target of terror in order to produce disorientation and/or compliance, or to mobilize secondary targets of demands (e.g., a government) or targets of attention (e.g., public opinion). (p. 111)[3]

This definition has many advantages (Ross, 1988a, 1988b), and with four qualifications it is relatively appropriate. First, not every element of the definition (e.g., method of combat) must exist for an action or campaign to be labeled terrorist. Second, though terrorism sometimes appears random in its targeting, it may actually be selective (e.g., directed against particular groups).[4] Third, violent attacks on symbolic, nonhuman targets (e.g., statues, buildings) that meet the definitional criteria are also considered acts of terrorism.[5] And fourth, only acts that have a declared political motive can justifiably be defined as terrorist acts (e.g., Hacker, 1976). Conversely, events that are mainly "criminal" in nature (e.g., extortion) or acts committed by psychologically "abnormal" people and that are not politically motivated are not included in the broad category of terrorism.[6]

	Direct involvement of nationals of more than one state	No direct involvement of nationals of more than one state
Government controlled or directed	Interstate/ state-sponsored terrorism	State terrorism
Not government controlled or directed	International/ transnational terrorism	Domestic terrorism

Figure 5.1   Typology of Political Terrorism: Involvement of Nationals of One or More States
Source: Mickolus, 1981.

TYPOLOGIES

Several different types of oppositional terrorism (i.e., domestic, state-sponsored, and international) exist (e.g., Mickolus, 1981). Thus, it seems logical that each kind has a slightly different pattern of causation and that the relative importance of each contributing factor varies according to the type of terrorist act, the group that commits it, and its location in space and time.

Jongman (1983), for example, outlines roughly 10 bases for classifying different types of terrorism; lists five alternative definitions of international terrorism put forward by various authors; and focuses on the following typologies: actor based, politically oriented, multidimensional, and purpose based. The first typology distinguishes between state and nonstate actors. The second differentiates between terrorism from above or below, and between right-wing and left-wing terrorism. The third subsumes distinctions based on Thornton's (1964) and Bell's (1978) work. Jongman concludes that "one of the problems with typology building is the absence of a commonly agreed-upon definition of terrorism," then constructs an actor-based typology using the state and the nonstate participants as the major actors.

HISTORICAL PERSPECTIVE

Terrorism, both a political and a violent crime, is not a new phenomenon. It has a long, rich history that can be classified into three time periods: *ancient, modern*, and *contemporary* (e.g., Laqueur, 1977; Vetter & Pearlstein, 1991; Wardlaw, 1982). It is generally the different types of tactics and issues that distinguish one epoch from another.

The period of *ancient terrorism* occurred in the years between A.D. 66 and 1870. Three major groups were active then: the Sicarri (A.D. 66-73), the Assassins (11th-12th centuries), and the Boxers (1905).[7] The dominance of these three terrorist organizations "lasted longer than any contemporary terror-ist group . . . and [was] responsible for much greater destruction than their more modern counterparts. Their activity, in contrast to the essentially secular con-temporary movements was . . . religious in character" (Taylor, 1988, p. 38).

Modern terrorism occurred between 1871 and 1960. Several organi-zations operated, including the Narodnya Volya, anarchist groups, the Social Revolutionary Party, and radical national-separatist groups in Ireland, Macedonia, Serbia, and Armenia. During the earliest part of this period, the lion's share had leftist sentiments and a fleeting existence.

> [A]fter World War I terrorist operations were mainly sponsored by right-wing and separatist groups. Sometimes these groups were both right-wing and separatist, as in the case of the Croatian Ustacha, which received most of its support from Fascist Italy and Hungary. . . . Systematic terrorism was found in the 1920s mainly on the fringes of the budding Fascist movements or among their precursors such as the Freikorps in Germany, certain French Fascist groups, in Hungary and, above all the Rumanian "Iron Guard." (Laqueur, 1977, p. 17)

Contemporary terrorism has taken place from roughly 1960 to the present. Since at least 1968, there has been an increase in both the number of inci-dents and the number of terrorist groups formed in advanced industrialized democracies. During this period terrorist acts became more violent (as measured by number of individuals injured or killed). New groups that emerged after the 1960s were better organized than their historical prede-cessors. Likewise, terrorism during this time has been better documented and researched and, consequently, public awareness has been heightened about this type of activity.

There are four important differences distinguishing terrorism of the con-temporary period from previous eras. First, "most of the terrorist groups of the 1960s were left-wing in orientation or, in any case, used left-wing phrase-ology in their appeals and manifestos." Second, "foreign powers, directly or discreetly . . . provided help to terrorist movements." Third, "operations in third countries became far more frequent." And fourth, "the ability of authorities to counteract terrorism was more restricted than in the past" (Laqueur, 1977, pp. 176-177). Consequently, international terrorism has increased dramatically.

Advanced industrialized democracies have been the political and economic systems most frequently targeted by oppositional terrorism during the contemporary period. Groups that have engaged in such anti-regime terrorism have subscribed to a wide spectrum of ideologies. Terrorism has existed throughout the history of most of the advanced industrialized countries, but it was most prominent in these political and economic systems during the 1960s and 1970s.

HOW WIDESPREAD IS THE PROBLEM?

Prior to the mid-1970s, the majority of information on terrorism was presented in case studies of individuals, groups, and particular movements that used terrorism, and on countries that experienced this type of political crime. This material was generally descriptive, atheoretical, and normative. In the mid-1970s, however, there was a greater attempt by scholars, private research corporations, and governmental departments to collect data systematically on the actions and characteristics of terrorism. These efforts led to quantitative studies that, unlike the descriptive analyses, allow greater precision in conveying the frequency of terrorism and testing hypotheses (Ross, 1991).

The most widely used data sources are the Control Risks Data Base, the RAND Corporation Data Base, and the State Department (CIA) data set (Ross, 1991). Although these data sets suffer from a number of problems (Ross, 1991), in particular their exclusive focus on international/transnational political terrorism, for the purposes of this chapter, statistics are based on information from State Department documents (e.g., http://www.state.gov/s/ct/rls/pgf.rpt).[8]

Number of Events/Annual Trends

The prevailing impression given by the mass media, public officials, and experts concerned with international terrorism is that it is on the increase. For the most part, the increase in terrorism is real rather than an artifact created by both better media and academic attention. From 1981 to 2001 there were a total of 9,542 international terrorist events, ranging from a low of 274 incidents in 1998 to a high of 666 in 1987. However, the increase has not been linear, as media accounts might imply. Over the past two-and-a-half decades there has been a ragged increase with several peaks and valleys. This is not surprising; throughout history terrorism has frequently occurred in cyclical upsurges, due partly to general factors involved in causation and decline. In 2001, the most recent year for which statistics are available, the total number of international terrorist incidents leveled off at 348, which is 78 fewer events than in 2000, and the fifth lowest in the past decade. However, not all events are of the same magnitude and intensity. For example, the September 11, 2001, attacks on the World Trade Center and the Pentagon might lead to the conclusion that there has been a steep increase in terrorism, which on closer examination has not occurred.

Geographic Spread

The increase in the volume of terrorist activity has been matched by its geographic spread. The number of countries experiencing some sort of terrorist activity each year has gradually increased. In the late 1960s, international terrorist incidents occurred in an average of 29 countries each year. This number climbed to 39 countries in the early 1970s and 43 in the late 1970s. For the first 3 years of the 1980s, the average number of countries experiencing international terrorist incidents was 51, and for the period from 1983 to 1985, it was 65.

Although terrorism is experienced throughout the world, a considerable number of states currently experience a disproportionate amount of the world's terrorism. About 20 countries account for between 75% and 90% of all reported incidents. The three states experiencing the largest amount of terrorism (approximately 75% of the total) are, in descending order of frequency, Israel (including the Gaza Strip and the West Bank), Pakistan, and Columbia.

Despite the fact that regions experiencing the greatest amount of terrorism change each year, in 1988 the largest number of events took place in the Middle East with 313 incidents, followed by Asia with 194 incidents, then Western Europe with 149 actions. By 2001, Latin America received the brunt of terrorist *attacks* occurring between 1995 and 2001. On the other hand, during this same period, Africa incurred the greatest number of *casualties*.

Targets

Over the past 30 years, the spectrum of terrorist targets has expanded. At the beginning of the 1970s, terrorists concentrated their attacks mainly on property/institutions, whereas in the 1980s they increasingly directed their targeting against people. Almost every conceivable structure has been hit (e.g., embassies, factories, airliners, airline offices, tourist agencies, hotels, airports, bridges, trains, train stations, reactors, refineries, schools, restaurants, pubs, churches, temples, synagogues, computers in large businesses and organizations, data-processing centers, and office towers). A considerable amount of attention has been directed toward the possibility of terrorist attacks on nuclear facilities and the potential fallout that would take place. Indeed, there have been breaches of security at these places; however, most of the incidents were carried out by anti-nuclear activists and were aimed at halting or delaying the construction of nuclear facilities rather than at the destruction of existing ones. Between 1996 and 2001, the principal targets attacked were military (48), government (90), diplomatic (197), miscellaneous (547), and businesses (1,902).

Americans, French, Israelis, British, and Turks account for approximately half of all the nationalities victimized by terrorists. Some of the people who have been attacked include diplomats, military personnel, tourists, businesspeople, students, journalists, children, nuns, priests, and the Pope. According to State Department statistics, since 1996 the majority of victims or facilities that were targeted are miscellaneous (4,496). Otherwise, in descending order of frequency, victims or facilities include business (2,552), diplomatic (2,347), governmental (958), and military (747).

Between 1996 and 2001 there were a total of 17,632 casualties inflicted by international terrorism. By the end of 2001, largely because of the September 11 bombings of the World Trade Center and the Pentagon, and the hijacking and crashing of another airplane in rural Pennsylvania, allegedly committed by members of al Qaeda, the number of casualties rose to 4,655. Typically, only 15% to 20% of all terrorist incidents involve fatalities, and of those, 66% involve only one death. Less than 1% of the thousands of terrorist incidents that have occurred in the past two decades involved 10 or more fatalities; incidents of mass murder, sometimes achieved through suicide bombings, are truly rare. This has led some commentators to suggest that terrorists want a lot of people watching rather than a lot of people dying. This perspective might be called into question as a result of the current spate of suicide bombings in Israel.

Tactics

Terrorists operate with a fairly limited repertoire of attacks. Six basic tactics have accounted for 95% of all terrorist incidents: bombings, assassinations, armed assaults, kidnappings, hijackings, and barricade and hostage incidents. In short, terrorists blow things up, kill people, or seize hostages. Every terrorist incident is essentially a variation on these three activities.

Bombings of all types continue to be the most popular terrorist method of attack. Approximately 50% of all international terrorist events are bombings. This is followed, in terms of numbers, by armed attacks, arsons, and kidnappings. In addition, assassinations, bombings, arsons, and attacks on diplomats have increased in the past few years.

Though the majority of bombs are simple incendiary devices, terrorists have made and often used more sophisticated explosive devices. Finally, terrorist use of weapons of mass destruction, such as nuclear, chemical, biological, or toxic weapons is a topic of constant concern.

Terrorist Groups

Most of the currently active terrorist groups show no sign of abandoning their struggle. Some of them have been working for a decade or more replacing their losses, preparing for new attacks, and turning into semi-permanent subcultures.

In 1991, Crenshaw examined the longevity of 76 terrorist organizations. Many exhibited remarkable stability and tenacity, but almost half of the organizations that existed at some time no longer exist or no longer use terrorism. However, at least 10 groups have been in operation for 20 years (including Al-Fatah, the Popular Front for the Liberation of Palestine-General Command (PFLPGC), Euzkadi Ta Askatasuna (ETA), and others) (Crenshaw, 1991).

Notably, some of the new organizations (Hamas, al Qaeda) formed in the 1980s are now taking their struggles international. Finally, terrorism is increasingly being committed by hardened (criminally, psychologically, and socially) but inexperienced youth with their own agendas. Thus, in many respects terrorist groups often resemble street gangs found in some of the large inner cities in America.

RESEARCH AND THEORETICAL IMPLICATIONS

One enigma emerging out of terrorism research is the overabundance of descriptions and the relative dearth of empirical causal studies.[9] Needless to say, the most prominent theoretical explanations are structural, social-psychological, and rational choice.[10] In an effort to explain the dynamics of terrorism, this chapter reviews the structural and social-psychological explanations by consolidating five principal structural factors. Variables that are logically connected and amenable to empirical testing are outlined. These factors include a complex array of processes derived from research descriptive of and associated with the dynamics of terrorism. There is considerable diversity among terrorists and their organizations, but if analyses are to move beyond case studies, we need to formulate hypotheses, collect better data, and test the propositions that we have developed.

As a general proposition, the higher the number of and intensity of structural and social-psychological causes of terrorism (the independent variables), the greater the number of terrorist acts perpetrated for any particular terrorist or organization (the dependent variable). If these factors are causally related, then the systematic elimination or lessening of them should lead to a decrease in terrorism.

CAUSES

Few researchers have developed a general model or theory of the causes of terrorism. More common are studies that list several possible factors but fail to specify their interactions. However, there are five well-known attempts to create or test structural theories and models of terrorism or to explain the processes of the political offense that merit attention (e.g., Crenshaw, 1981; Gross, 1972; Hamilton, 1978; Johnson, 1982, chap. 8; Targ, 1979).

Although these authors produced a highly important knowledge base from which to conduct further study, they have a number of difficulties

(Ross, 1993a, 1994, 1996, 1999). The benefits of the previous works on the causes of terrorism are maximized by specifying causal relationships between variables.

A phenomenal body of literature on the psychological causes of terrorism reflects several research strategies. First, there is a series of case studies of individual terrorists (e.g., Bollinger, 1981; Caplan, 1983; Kelman, 1983; Knutson, 1981). Second, there are a number of studies of terrorist groups or subtypes thereof (e.g., Clark, 1983; Hubbard, 1971; IJOGT, 1982a, 1982b; Morf, 1970; Russell & Miller, 1983; Weinberg & Eubank, 1987). Third, and closely connected to analyses of certain terrorist groups, are psychological interpretations of terrorism that are place/country specific (e.g., Ferracuti & Bruno, 1981). Fourth, a considerable amount of research ascribes the psychological causes to one or two theoretical explanations (e.g., Caplan, 1983; Crayton, 1983; Crenshaw, 1990a; Ferracuti, 1982; Gutmann, 1979; McCauley & Segal, 1987; Miron, 1976; Morf, 1970; Pearlstein, 1991). Fifth, some literature primarily critiques other research (e.g., Corrado, 1981; Crenshaw, 1990b; Reich, 1990). Finally, by far the majority of work consists of literature reviews (e.g., Cooper, 1977; Crenshaw, 1985; Hacker, 1976; Hubbard, 1971, 1983; Margolin, 1977; Taylor, 1988).

Various problems also plague psychological explanations of terrorism, including, but not limited to, the relevance of causes, assumptions that terrorism is different from other types of violent political or criminal behavior, use of psychological explanations of terrorism, psychological health of terrorists, methodologies used for psychological studies of terrorism, contribution of nonpsychological causes to the commission of terrorism, and tradeoffs between overgeneralization and reductionism (Ross, 1994). None of these criticisms, however, eliminates the utility of continued theorizing about and research on the psychological causes of terrorism.

Although this information has contributed to our knowledge of terrorism, there is no grand theory that can explain why terrorists do what they do and who will become a terrorist. Because each type of terrorism has a different pattern of causation, the relative importance of each independent variable depends on the context, including the type of perpetrator, terrorist act, target, country, and time period.[11] A broad theoretical framework that can accommodate some of these ideas may be achieved through integrating both structural and psychological explanations.

Structural Explanations

There are at least 10 structural explanations of terrorism. In general, most of these factors act as independent variables while occasionally acting as dependent factors in causal ordering. Following Crenshaw's (1985) distinction, these explanations may be divided into permissive and precipitant causes. Regardless of the complexity of the command structure and the size of the organization, acts of terrorism may be carried out by individuals alone or as group members.

At the core of the precipitant causes are the permissive factors that are endemic to all societies. Permissive causes also are considered to be systemic conditions that prestructure and facilitate the presence of the precipitants. The three permissive causes are geographical location, type of political system, and amount of modernization. These three factors are necessary but not sufficient interacting predecessors to create conditions for terrorism.

Precipitant causes are the final triggering mechanisms that motivate people and organizations to engage in terrorism. The most common precipitants are social, cultural, and historical facilitation; organizational split and development; presence of other forms of unrest; support; counter-terrorist organization failure; availability of weapons and explosives; and grievances (Ross, 1993a).

The permissive causes should structure the type and frequency of precursors to a group's choice of terrorism, which is facilitated by precipitant causes that are interactive. Even though the seven precipitants may motivate individuals or groups to choose terrorism for obtaining their goals, typically the pattern is more complex. For example, grievances can lead to support, which in turn may lead to grievances or the availability of weapons and explosives. Counterterrorist organization failure can lead to support; and organizational split and development may lead to grievances.[12]

Social-Psychological Explanations

In general, there are five interconnected processes that social-psychological theories explain: joining, forming, remaining in, and leading a terrorist organization; and engaging in terrorist actions. Although people can engage in politically violent acts alone, the process of committing terrorism is aided by belonging to or leading a terrorist group, and the frequency of one's violent acts likely increases if conducted in a group setting and with organizational support. This interpretation is complementary with differential association theory, which would allow that terrorism, like any other crime, is learned behavior reinforced by socialization into the group.

Seven psychological theories explain terrorists' behavior: psychoanalytical (e.g., Morf, 1970); learning (e.g., Pitcher & Hamblin, 1982), frustration-aggression (e.g., Gurr, 1970); narcissism-aggression (e.g., Pearlstein, 1991); trait (Russell & Miller, 1983); developmental (Sayari, 1985); and motivational/rational choice (e.g., Crenshaw, 1990a). These theories are accepted as partial explanations because none is in and of itself a sufficient social-psychological cause of terrorism. An alternative strategy proposed here is to integrate them into a single approach.[13]

According to an integrated view, childhood and adolescent experiences condition individuals to develop personality traits that predispose them to engage in terrorism (Ross, 1994, 1996). The development of these facilitating traits can be explained by either psychoanalytic, learning, frustration, or narcissism-aggression theories. The relevant traits motivate people either to commit terrorism alone; form bonds with other people who are predisposed to engage in terrorism; or sometimes to develop, join, remain in, or lead terrorist organizations. Terrorists experience their most important learning opportunities within the group they belong to. These experiences, in turn, shape the cost-benefit calculus of individual terrorists.

Ultimately, the choice to engage in a terrorist action is a conscious or unconscious rational choice decision, sometimes referred to as an expression of political strategy where expected utility is calculated by individual terrorists and collectively by terrorist groups (e.g., Crenshaw, 1990a).[14] In other words, terrorists engage in their behaviors because they are relatively rational human beings and not because they suffer from psychological maladjustments (e.g., Corrado, 1981).

Examinations of terrorists' motivations show well thought-out logic for their behavior (e.g., Kaplan, 1978). According to some terrorists, their actions are a cost-effective means to achieve individual, collective, tangible, or symbolic recognition, attention, or publicity for their cause; disrupt and discredit a government or other appropriate target; create fear and/or hostility in an audience identified as the "enemy"; provoke a counterrevolution by the government; create sympathy or acceptance among potential supporters; and increase control, discipline, and morale building within the terrorist group (e.g., Hacker, 1976).

Rational choices are linked to the objectives of the terrorist act. In this sense, terrorist practices appear rational (perhaps bounded),[15] because they are committed in order to meet a set of political purposes and goals. These objectives include: "to terrify"; "advertis[e] a cause"; "provo[ke]"; and "raise . . . morale along with that of whatever group in whose name they claim to be acting by disclosing the vulnerability of their enemies"; "or, if the victims belong to some disliked group (e.g., foreign business people) . . . [encourage] admiration for their deed among the general population"; and "sustain . . . the group that is responsible for the violence" (Weinberg & Davis, 1989, pp. 9-10). It has been argued that the greater the sophistication, as measured by planning, target selection, and risk, the higher the level of rational choice involved in the process.

> Terrorists may . . . perform activities they believe are likely to win wide-spread approval from their selected audiences . . . [and] desist from activities that are too brutal or too difficult to justify on ethical grounds. Terrorists may also fear that inactivity will cause them to lose credibility, support, or the chance to gain new recruits—and that people within the terrorist organization will become restless or depressed. (Jenkins, 1982, pp. 61-62)

SUMMARY

Terrorist attacks are disruptive to the normal functioning of people's daily routines, business, and government organization. In terms of political crime, terrorism has been a very prominent aspect of modern living. The specter of terrorism has political cache in news headlines and among holiday travelers. And if the events of September 11, 2001, are any indication, terrorism will be with us indefinitely.

NOTES

1. Unless otherwise indicated, all further references to terrorism subsume oppositional and political components.

2. Oppositional political terrorism is conducted by anti-state and anti-corporate individuals and organizations. There are two types of oppositional terrorism—domestic

and international-transnational. Domestic terrorism occurs at a greater frequency than international. Oppositional terrorism contrasts with state terrorism (see Chapters 6-8), which is carried out by government agencies against real or suspected threats to the regime.

3. Assassination generally is the work of an individual or organization to kill a person and whose goal, unlike terrorism, is primarily simply to eliminate the person rather than to threaten others. Sabotage involves damaging property; if the property is government owned or contributes to the security of a country, then the action has an explicit political context. The majority of academic literature that examines this practice discusses sabotage in the context of war or war-like conditions and argues against its political content. Because of their highly contextual nature, neither assassination nor sabotage will be addressed in this book.

4. This recognizes that terrorists make cost-benefit calculations regarding targets and methods, which mitigates the perception or charge of randomness.

5. Terrorist activities are often directed first against nonhuman targets and progress to human targets. Most databases on terrorism include this distinction as well as threats and hoaxes.

6. In 1988, Schmid revised his consensus definition. Despite his efforts to improve upon his previous efforts, many analysts prefer the old definition over the new one. This state of affairs may be more a reflection of the tolerance of those for answering these kinds of surveys.

7. The political content of the Thugs is highly questionable (see, e.g., Vetter & Pearlstein, 1991, p. 31).

8. The State Department, through the Office of the Ambassador at Large for Counter-Terrorism, issues an annual "Patterns of Global Terrorism" report (e.g., http://www.state.gov/s/ct/rls/pgf.rpt). When appropriate State Department information was not available, RAND reports were relied on.

9. For a review of the merits and limitations of the literature on oppositional political terrorism in the United States and Canada, respectively, see Ross (1988a, 1988b, 1993b).

10. Reilly (1973) makes the same point with regard to internal war. Romano (1984) divides the causes into the biological, psychiatric, and sociological schools; Mitchell (1985) identifies ideologies, the environment, and individual factors; Turk (1982b) describes criminological approaches to terrorism; and Keenan (1987) outlines sociological and psychological explanations.

11. Perpetrator characteristics include, for example, age, gender, and ideology (e.g., anarchist, communist, nationalist, separatist, and right-wing; Post, 1986). Regarding terrorist acts, several types of oppositional terrorism are recognized (e.g., domestic, international, state-sponsored), and even finer differentiations could be made with different geographic and actor dimensions.

12. For further details of structural explanations, see Ross (1993a).

13. Integrating these theories is difficult, especially because they have fundamentally different underlying logics.

14. This position is not unanimously held. For further coverage of psychological explanations see Post (1990) and Ross (1994, 1996).

15. For an explanation of this concept see Simon (1982).

TEST QUESTIONS

Multiple-Choice

1. Who were the Sicarri?
    a. Praetorians
    b. people who used hashish in their ceremonies
    c. terrorists who operated during the ancient period
    d. theorists who integrated case studies and cross-national research
    e. Russian terrorists

2. What is the most important structural cause of oppositional political terrorism?
    a. type of political system
    b. location
    c. availability of weapons
    d. grievances
    e. support

3. Who, among the following, developed explanations for the structural causes of oppositional political terrorism?
    a. Crenshaw
    b. Gurr
    c. Kellett
    d. Mickolus
    e. Turk

4. What type of political terrorism do most databases on this subject examine?
    a. domestic
    b. state sponsored
    c. ideological
    d. transnational
    e. corporate

5. Who developed a consensus definition of terrorism?
   a. Ross
   b. Tilly
   c. Schmid
   d. Taylor
   e. Mickolus

6. According to the literature, are most terrorists suffering from some form of psychopathology?
   a. yes
   b. no
   c. depends on the sophistication of the evaluation technique
   d. only those who get captured
   e. only the anarchists

7. What were three major terrorist groups operating between 1871 and 1960?
   a. Sicarri, Assassins, and Boxers
   b. Crazies, Criminals, and Crusaders
   c. Macedonians, Serbians, and Armenians
   d. Anarchists, Socialists, and Communists
   e. none of the above

Short Answer

1. Why is it important to study the causes of terrorism?

2. What are seven structural causes of oppositional political terrorism?

3. What are five psychological theories that have contributed to the understanding of oppositional political terrorism?

4. Provide a critical analysis of Mickolus's typology.

※ SIX ※

STATE CRIME

———•◦•———

U ntil recently, the majority of research on crime has focused on the illegal actions of individuals and organizations (i.e., gangs, syndicates, and corporations). Less attention has been given to state crimes (Ross et al., 1999). When crimes of the state, also known as governmental lawlessness (Sykes & Cullen, 1992, p. 269), and a subset of "crimes of the powerful" (Box, 1983; Pearce, 1976) are addressed, they are largely treated as a consequence of or a response to insurgent violence, perceived threats to national security, or simply the behaviors of authoritarian regimes in Second (transitional) and Third World (less developed) countries. They are rarely portrayed as the normal everyday functioning of governments in their desire to maintain power.

Since the late 1980s, however, a growing number of criminologists have pointed out the role of the state in the commission and facilitation of crimes. They recognize that state crime is pervasive and committed with varying frequency by all types of countries, from democracy to totalitarian, from capitalist to communist (Barak, 1990, 1991; Friedrichs, 1998a, 1998b; Grabosky, 1989; Ross, 1995/2000, 2000d). Moreover, the state often is the initiator rather than simply the mediator or target of the crime.

One of the nagging questions is why it took so long for criminologists to focus on the problem of state crime. As Barak (1993) suggested, it was at least two decades after Sutherland's groundbreaking examination of white-collar crime before social scientists turned their attention to the crimes of the privately powerful. Now, more than three decades after social scientists of the early 1970s delineated state crimes, attention is finally being given to the

BOX 6.1 Gregg Barak (1948-)

Barak was born on June 29, 1948, in Los Angeles, California. He received his Doctorate in Criminology in 1974 from the University of California, Berkeley. He has held teaching positions at six universities and administrative positions at three, most recently as head of the Department of Sociology, Anthropology, and Criminology at Eastern Michigan University (1991-1996). He is currently a Professor of Criminology and Criminal Justice at EMU. He is the author or editor of 10 books, including the award winning *Gimme Shelter: A Social History of Homelessness in Contemporary America* (1991); *Crimes by the Capitalist State: An Introduction to State Criminality* (1991); *Integrating Criminologies* (1998); *Media, Criminal Justice, and Mass Culture* (2nd ed., 1999); and most recently, *Crime and Crime Control: A Global View* (2000), and *Class, Race, Gender, and Crime: Social Realities of Justice in America* (2001).

Barak has been a member of the board or officer, including president, of various shelters or programs for the homeless, hungry, or sexually abused and assaulted. In the field of political crime he is best known for his book on state crime, *Crimes by the Capitalist State,* and for tracing the political implications of state policies on crime. To find out more about Professor Barak and his work, and to read such topical essays of his as "Transnational Crime" and "Comparative Crime and Justice," visit his Web site at www.greggbarak.com.

misdeeds of the publicly powerful. In general, perhaps because of the controversial nature of state crimes, it takes a while for scholars to accept certain topics for legitimate study.

Apparently, no state is immune from using such repressive tactics when its managers and agents define people or groups as threatening to social, political, or economic order. This position is coterminous with the three basic interpretations of the role of the state.[1]

Although private institutions wield coercive power, the state holds the exclusive legal authority to coerce. In fact, theorists from Marx through Weber to Mann have noted the importance of both coercion and criminality to state power. State crime has existed since the formation of the first country, and it has been suggested that it may, in fact, be necessary for the very creation of states (Gurr, 1988).

The notion of the state and/or those employed by it committing crimes is not new. Mills (1956, chap. 13) explains the notion he calls "higher immorality." Here he is talking about criminal or unethical actions by

> the upper levels of the nation's corporate, political and military elite. The structural basis of the higher immorality finds that institutionalized forms of corruption often involve interrelated scandals. Events in one major scandal are often linked to events in one or more additional scandals. Some of the same players in one scandal are involved in one or another debacle. (Mills as cited in Hagan, 1997, pp. 87-88)

Indeed, scholars, jurists, and the public have questioned academics about their broad use of the term *state crime* (e.g., Sharkansky, 1995). The concept is useful, and with cautious operationalization it helps us explain the misdeeds of government institutions and agencies, powerful individuals acting in the name of the state, and those acting criminally due to the state power with which they have been vested.

HOW WIDESPREAD IS THE PROBLEM?

There are several practical problems with monitoring state criminality: It is often difficult to detect; it is hard to prosecute people accused of perpetrating these acts; it is hard to pin the crime on the appropriate person; and those charged often have considerable resources to mount a sustained defense. In particular, most nonviolent state crimes go undetected because of the ability of the perpetrators to engage in cover-ups (i.e., hiding incriminating or critical evidence or documentation), to destroy documentation, and/or to engineer the disappearance of critical witnesses.

Nonviolent state crimes, sometimes referred to as political repression or the quelling of dissent, are not easily categorized (Parenti, 1995, pp. 139-142; Wolfe, 1973). The 1972 Watergate scandal, for example, was discovered only by accident when a security guard stumbled upon "the Plumbers," people breaking into the Democratic National Headquarters (Woodward & Bernstein, 1974).

Those being investigated for state crimes often have considerable resources that allow them to divert or stall investigative inquiries. Many try to claim that their actions were committed in the name of national security, or they rely on "plausible deniability" as their defense.

State crimes are typically committed by people in positions of power, and they occur more often than we realize. Rarely are incidents of state malfeasance brought to public attention. Why? Typically, these actions are hidden or covered up to avoid embarrassment for both the person committing the act and the agency that employs the person. Alternatively, such crimes are hard to trace because of solidarity among government workers in tight-knit groups (e.g., police, military). Unless one of them has a grudge against another, or has an overly moral conscience, many bureaucrats will look the other way when they see or hear about deviant actions occurring in their place of employment to avoid being perceived as disloyal to coworkers and superiors in their agency. Even when those questionable acts or state crimes come to public attention (and rarely are citizens given the full story) through the media or governmental inquiries, the facts can be skewed or biased. Either the agency tries its best to cover up the crime, representatives engage in plausible deniability, there is considerable red tape the investigator must wade through, or the investigator is limited by having to deal with the offender in a very secretive manner. Alternatively, state crimes that do come to public attention, like death squad activity in Panama, Chile, and Peru, are explained by state officials as parts of "raison d'etat"—the right of the state to engage in affairs on its own soil.

As for politicians committing a crime, they may be fortunate enough to bribe officials or call in old favors to get a lighter sanction or even to avoid punishment altogether.

DEFINITIONAL AND CONCEPTUAL ISSUES

Central questions emerge when contemplating state crime, including, but not limited to, "What is the State?" "How did it form?" "What is its nature?" and "How does state crime change over time?" Understanding these concepts is essential to the discussion of who has the power to implement policies in government, and why particular actions are taken by state employees. Most important for our discussion, these questions clarify the notion of state crime. Before continuing it is probably helpful to distinguish among the terms that many of us take for granted but that are important for this discussion: nation, country, and state.

A nation consists of people who share a common history, language, race, and culture but who do not necessarily live in the same geographic location (e.g., Armenians, Palestinians). A country is land that has discernable borders. In general, states have population, territory, government, and sovereignty (Khan & McNiven, 1991, pp. 26-34). According to most state theorists and critical criminologists, the state is the political entity that holds a legitimate monopoly on the use of force, law, and administration. The state holds the balance of power in any political conflict. Why? It has a disproportionate amount of resources in order to carry out this mandate. Any understanding of the contemporary advanced industrialized democratic country is best served by recognizing that the state has not always existed and is typically a product of conflict (Engels, 1942; Tilly, 1985).[2] To maintain power, states (and by extension, regimes) must achieve and sustain legitimacy.[3] This approach is highly relevant to theories of power and interest articulation.[4]

POWER AND INTEREST ARTICULATION

Three interpretations or "faces" of power provide separate but interrelated explanations concerning the role of government and its purpose in society. The views (not power), it can be argued, are products of their time and thus have been challenged and modified over time (e.g., Alford & Friedland, 1986; Etzioni-Halevy, 1989).

In the 1960s, the theoretical notion of pluralism was developed (Dahl, 1961; Polsby, 1980). Pluralism, also known as the "first face of power," argued that in the political arena everyone has an equal chance of being heard, and that majorities prevail and have their policy preferences enacted. Theorists and researchers working in this tradition argued that the state is a neutral entity, a "black box," that exists simply to translate the will of the people into policies, legislation, and practices. The state implements the "will of the people," which is expressed through conventional political participation (e.g., voting, supporting politicians and political parties). Pluralists believed that society demonstrates their wishes, and government responds to and serves their needs. They argued that the reason so few people participate in the political process (usually referred to as apathy) is because of their lack

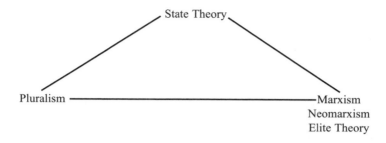

Figure 6.1 Outline of the Three Faces of Power

of interest in politics. In short, pluralism had a considerable amount of resonance among the American public because this is what American school-children are taught to believe, especially the notion that every vote counts (see Figure 6.1).

During the late 1960s, as both an intellectual reaction to the short-comings of pluralist theory and a social response to the events that were taking place in advanced industrialized democracies (e.g., anti-war demonstrations, race riots, student movements, demands for the expansion of civil rights), the elite (Domhoff, 1983; Mills, 1956), Marxist, and neo-Marxist theories evolved (Bachrach & Baratz, 1962; Parenti, 1995). Those who advocated this position, which is also known as the "second face of power," argued that not everyone has the same access to power and not all people can participate. Moreover, those who have a disproportionate amount of resources (e.g., the owners and managers of the means of production) are typically the ones who participate politically. Unfortunately for the powerless in society, it is the elite's agenda that is too often translated into policies and laws. Coterminous with this explanation is Bachrach and Baratz's idea of "mobilization of bias." This generally occurs when elite interests can prevent certain groups and issues from reaching the political agenda. "Mobilization of bias" specifically refers to the practice whereby large powerful entities use their resources to frustrate the wishes of the majority. Opportunities for confrontation are structured so that the political ideas or desires of the less powerful do not come to the table and/or are not aired in public. Only the strongest and most influential people in our society affect the government. This theory purports that government serves only the affluent and upper-class members.

Finally, in the 1980s, a third variant, called state theory, developed (e.g., Carnoy, 1984; Skocpol, 1979). State theorists argued that even though the governments of advanced industrialized democracies are run by elected or appointed officials, the most important political actor is the bureaucracy. Borrowing from the fields of public administration, public policy, and organizational behavior, they suggested that because the state has a disproportionate amount of resources, its workers and agents primarily carry out rules and laws in connection with their own views about how things should work. Government workers and administrators are primarily self-interested and thus are concerned with organizational maintenance and expansion. They will lobby citizens and legislatures on behalf of policies and practices they believe will help their agency, and those that will serve these narrow goals. Bureaucracies can also frustrate policies they believe are unfounded, threaten their agenda, or minimize their ability to showcase their skills or talents. Needless to say, the state can facilitate or frustrate political participation (Gaventa, 1980; Lukes, 1974). At the same time, interests can have a history of their own. Repeatedly frustrated in their political participation, workers and the general public become alienated and apathetic, leaving the decision making up to someone else.

CONCEPTUAL CLARIFICATION OF STATE CRIME

Turk (1982a, chap. 4), for example, distinguishes between acts committed against the government as "political crimes" and acts committed by the government or state as "political policing." Although Turk sensitizes us to the dichotomy between the two actions, it does not appear that he accords state crime the same legitimacy as oppositional political crimes. Perhaps this is why other writers use the term *political crime* as an umbrella concept for crimes both against and by the state (e.g., Gibbons, 1987; Michalowski, 1985; Thomas & Hepburn, 1983).

Some of the criminological community and much of society have adopted a double standard regarding definitions of the words *crime* and *criminal*. Crimes against the government (or society) have long been regarded as *real* crimes; that is, serious, harmful acts that are rightly criminalized and receive copious attention from the mass media (Barak, 1994). On the other hand, the abuse of power by the state is perceived as less egregious and is often designated as necessary action, which receives erratic public attention. There is no sustained appreciation for the vast harms resulting directly from the actions of government agencies and agents (Chomsky, 1973; Clinard & Quinney, 1978).

The state and its lawmakers, managers, and bureaucrats are not solely architects and enforcers of law, but are also significant players in law violations. Indeed, the state holds a unique position—it is both "a crime-regulating and crime-generating institution" (Barak, 1993, p. 209). With respect to the latter behavior, the state has committed such garden-variety crimes as violence and theft but also has participated in illegalities available only to those with official state authority and power. Or, as Clinard and Quinney (1978) have outlined: "Those who legislate and enforce the law—and determine what is to be regarded as legitimate—are in the position of violating the laws themselves without being criminally defined" (p. 144).

Given the realities of sovereignty and national security, most states, regardless of their ideological foundations or political-economic systems, seemingly could not survive without some form of secrecy, espionage, and deception (Ross, 1992). The question then becomes, when do such actions violate law, and whose law is being violated?

Organizational governmental crimes are considered to be those "committed with the support and encouragement of a formal organization and intended at least in part to advance" its goals (Coleman, 1985, p. 8). The crimes permeate the institution, as illegalities are deemed necessary and functional for the bureaucracy's agenda and mandate, and for continuing the dominant political-economic order. Such organizational support is the defining characteristic of these types of crimes, which are vastly different sociologically from those committed by individuals for their own personal gain.

Naturally there is some definitional confusion between the concepts "state crime" and "government crime." Although some analysts "treat state crime as a subtype of governmental crime, quite often these terms are used interchangeably" (Friedrichs, 1995, p. 53). To clarify,

> the term *state* refers to a political entity with a recognized sovereignty occupying a definite territory, whereas the term government refers to the political and administrative apparatus of such an entity. . . . Government may also refer to the administrative apparatus of lesser political entities, such as municipalities. The term state crime suggests crime committed on behalf of a state (federal or not), while the term governmental crime . . . can more

naturally be applied to crimes committed within a governmental context
on any level, and not necessarily on behalf of the state. (Friedrichs, 1995,
pp. 53-54)

He clarifies further: "Governmental crime will be used as a broad term for the
whole range of crimes committed in a governmental context." State crime
"activities," he goes on, are those actions "carried out by the state or on behalf
of some state agency," and political white-collar crime refers to "illegal activities carried out by officials and politicians for direct personal benefit"
(Friedrichs, 1995, p. 54). Because the term *state crime* is better known, it is
used for this discussion.

Although the appropriateness of the term is debatable (e.g., Sharkansky,
1995), state crimes should include "coverups, corruption, disinformation,
unaccountability, and violations of domestic and/or international laws. It also
includes those practices that, although they fall short of being officially
declared illegal, are perceived by the majority of the population as illegal or
socially harmful" (Ross, 1995/2000, pp. 6-7).

TYPOLOGIES

Henry (1991, p. 256), building on the philosophical and ideological belief that
a state has certain moral and ethical obligations to its citizenry, distinguishes
between state crimes of commission and those inactions of the state referred
to as crimes of omission.[5] Thus, we can define state crimes as those acts that
bring physical, material, or social harm to a state's citizens, a subgroup of
people, or people of other countries resulting from the actions or consequences
of government policy mediated through the practice of state agencies, whether
these harms are intentional or unintentional.

Other concepts have been applied to state crime. In some cases, state
illegalities are referred to as *state authority occupational crimes,* a term
reserved for individuals vested with particular state authority—the legal power
to "represent the force of state law in certain decisions" (Green, 1990, p. 149).
Such crimes are possible because of the privileges of state authority occupations and the legal force available to those with government-sanctioned power.
In other words, state authority occupational crimes are the misuse of legally
vested authority and force, which includes such acts as corruption, bribe taking,

police brutality, military crimes, and illegal domestic surveillance activities. Other labels found in the literature for this type of political crime include elite deviance (Simon & Eitzen, 1999) and occupational crime (Coleman, 1994, pp. 11-12). Friedrichs (1995, pp. 58, 60) uses the much broader term *governmental crime* as an umbrella concept under which falls "political corruption," which he terms "political white collar crime." Friedrich reserves the concept "governmental crime" for those actions carried out by the state and its agents for both organizational state goals and people's own personal benefits. State crimes, for Friedrich, are a subcategory of governmental crimes, consisting of "activities carried out by the state or on behalf of some state agency," while political white collar crimes are "illegal activities carried out by officials and politicians for direct personal benefit" (p. 54).

Undoubtedly, governmental crime is characterized by conceptual and typological confusion. Clarifying this conceptual messiness is an ongoing task.

This treatment of state crime incorporates acts that are *mala in se* and *mala prohibita,* as well as those behaviors that currently are not prohibited by criminal law. Although the appropriateness of states' responsibilities can be and historically have been debated, crimes of commission and omission as well as acts labeled governmental crime, state crime, and political white-collar crime can be included (Ross, 1995/2000, pp. 4-6).

Therefore, state crime includes such actions as cover-ups, disinformation, unaccountability, corruption, and violations of domestic and/or international law. Also embedded are those practices that, although falling short of being officially declared illegal, are considered socially injurious. This definition recognizes that legal systems are slow to enact legislation; are highly normative; and often reflect elite, class, and nonpluralistic interests (Barak, 1993; Bohm, 1993; Quinney, 1977; Ross, 1995/2000, p. 6; Schwendinger & Schwendinger, 1975; Sutherland, 1949b, pp. 511-515).

Activities that are much more egregious in terms of lost dollars, human lives, and injuries—corporate and governmental wrongdoings engaged in by the powerful—typically are not legislated as criminal and are beyond the purview of the crime control industry. For example, these crimes are codified in regulatory rather than criminal law: Politically motivated crimes committed by the dispossessed typically are also activities legislated as criminal, whereas politically motivated crimes committed by the powerful acting in corporate or state interests typically are not.

This inclusive treatment of state crime also addresses and mitigates criticisms from the Right that state crime theory rests largely on semantics and from the Left who occasionally use ambiguous and nonrigorous concepts and methods. Unlike oppositional political crimes, it is hard to differentiate between violent and nonviolent types of state crimes. For example, many human rights violations can have both violent and nonviolent subtypes.

THE RELEVANCE OF STATE REPRESSION

A number of acts of state crime, often labeled state repression, do not easily fit into standard classifications. Repression is typically intentional or unintentional acts (most of which appear legal) designed to suppress or silence individuals or groups to keep them from participating in the political process. For example, it is not illegal for the FBI to place a car in front of your house and watch you enter and exit. And in most jurisdictions, as long as the authorities do not enter your premises or step foot on your property, they can go through your garbage.

Not only have state agencies frustrated or disrupted the activities of dissenters by spying on them; executing warrants to search their homes, offices, or vehicles; threatening them or their loved ones with violence or loss of jobs, but they have arrested them under legally questionable charges (i.e., false prosecution) (e.g., Goldstein, 1978). When dissenters do spend time in jail, their bail may be purposely set high and their prosecution may be dragged out in an effort to exhaust their resources and emotions, thereby creating conditions in which it appears as if due process is denied. This is true for individuals as well as the organizations to which they belong or lead. Although a conviction may not be obtained, this has the effect of wearing the individuals and organizations down. American history is replete with examples where this phenomenon has taken place (Parenti, 1995, p. 139).

The American criminal justice system, for example, has a number of mechanisms that have been periodically and selectively used to impede the activities of possible and actual dissenters, including the use of the grand jury, the Internal Revenue Service (IRS), Immigration and Naturalization Service (INS), the State Department, and the use of incarceration. According to Parenti (1995), "Supposedly intended to weigh the state's evidence and protect the innocent from unjustifiable prosecution, the grand jury ends up doing whatever the prosecution wants. Grand juries have been used to conduct 'fishing expeditions' against persons with unconventional views" (p. 139). Most of these proceedings take place without the defendant present, and when defendants are given the opportunity to be present, they are generally denied counsel. Questions are asked by the prosecution, and evidence is presented that typically leads the assembled juries to err on the side of caution. In other words, juries tend to favor the arguments put forward by prosecutors and to vote a "true bill" or indictment.

The Internal Revenue Service has been accused of using its power to audit individuals and organizations selectively. Apparently this has been used against the Communist Party, the National Council of Churches, "the Black Panther Party, Students for a Democratic Society, gay rights advocates, environmental groups, journalists, liberal politicians, and many other politically oriented individuals, organizations, and publications" (Parenti, 1995, p. 140).

The Immigration and Naturalization Service is charged with monitoring immigrants and visitors to the United States. The federal legislation that they are responsible for enforcing allows them the power to deny entry to individuals whom they believe are threats to U.S. national security and civil society. This branch of the U.S. Department of Justice is given the authority "to exclude anyone who might be affiliated with communist, anarchist, or 'terrorist' groups, or engaged in activities 'prejudicial to the public interest' and harmful to 'national security'" (Parenti, 1995, p. 140). Countless professionals, including "prominent authors, artists, performers, journalists, scientists, and labor-union leaders from other countries have been denied the right to visit and address audiences in the United States" (Parenti, 1995, pp. 140-141).

The U.S. State Department, through its Office of Passport Control, has denied travel visas to Americans wishing to visit countries such as Cuba and other communist countries against which the United States has a trade embargo.

Finally, Americans and other citizens have been incarcerated for long periods of time because their activities were at odds with the dominant elite interests of the time, or because judges had the latitude to hand down extended sentences for minor (often misdemeanor) charges. These so-called legal lynchings were imposed on famed labor leader Eugene Debs, Martin Sostre, Reverend Ben Chavis, Frank Shuford, and members of the Black Panther Party (Parenti, 1995, pp. 144-145). Mention is in order of those currently incarcerated who, because of their political persuasions, are singled out for abuse by correctional institutions (Ross & Richards, 2002).

SUMMARY

This chapter has demonstrated the conceptual confusion and definitional issues surrounding state crimes. The following section contains five chapters that cover the interrelated practices of political corruption, illegal domestic surveillance, human rights violations, state violence, and state-corporate crime. Each represents a widely recognized and practiced type of state illegality. Political corruption is treated primarily as a form of individual-based state crime made possible by the status and occupational opportunities available to government bureaucrats and managers. Illegal domestic surveillance, human rights violations, and state-corporate crime are more complex. They are organizational state crimes where states or their agencies, acting as units, adopt policies that usually are secretive and often use illegal domestic surveillance and violations of human rights as ongoing standard operating procedures. State violence can be treated as both organizational and individual crime, depending on the circumstances of the events.

NOTES

1. There are three basic interpretations of the role of the state. First, early radical conflict theorists argued that the state enables the oppression of one class by another (i.e., instrumentalism). Second, others considered the state to have a degree of relative autonomy from the privileged class (i.e., structuralism). Today, the state is interpreted as maintaining particular social and economic relationships, but often with its own interests set by ruling specialists in law making, law enforcement, and administration (e.g., Block, 1977; Kasinitz, 1983; Poulantzas, 1973). State managers and bureaucrats often engage in political crimes for their and the state's benefit rather than simply for the benefit of capitalism as a system or individuals and social classes who pull the strings of state mangers (e.g., Domhoff, 1983).

2. In this context, the state is not only the elected government, but also opposition political party members and those individuals working in the public administration.

3. This is consistent with other theorists' conceptualizations of the state (e.g., Alford & Friedland, 1985).

4. Nation-states develop when nations desire to occupy a particular geographic territory and establish a government.

5. A crime of omission is similar, in many respects, to what is generally known as "deliberate indifference."

TEST QUESTIONS

Multiple-Choice

1. Who among the following developed the first definition of state crime?
   a. Barak
   b. Gurr
   c. Grabosky
   d. Marx
   e. Ziegler

2. In which century has there been the greatest amount of state crime?
   a. 17th
   b. 18th
   c. 19th
   d. 20th
   e. the data are not yet comprehensive enough to determine this

3. Which author is the most adamant about the problems with the concept of state crime?
   a. Friedrichs
   b. Gill
   c. Menzies
   d. Ross
   e. Sharkansky

4. What is one of the most widely publicized and accepted types of state crime?
   a. terrorism
   b. political corruption
   c. human rights violations
   d. revolution
   e. war

5. Which of the following statements is true?
    a. state crime has existed since the creation of the first country
    b. state crime is a relatively new phenomenon
    c. most criminologists accept the concept of state crime
    d. most text books on criminology have a section on state crime
    e. none of the above

6. Which of the following is true about state crime?
    a. it is difficult to define
    b. it is hard to find appropriate data
    c. it is difficult to identify a single individual on whom to pin the crime
    d. the state has a disproportionate amount of resources to delay and sidetrack an investigation of state crime
    e. all of the above

7. Which political scientist is most closely associated with state theory?
    a. Dahl
    b. Parenti
    c. Ross
    d. Skocpol
    e. Turk

Short Answers

1. Define repression.

2. Give three examples of repression.

3. What is the most important "face of power" and why?

4. Explain Henry's typology.

⊰ SEVEN ⊱

POLITICAL CORRUPTION

———•◦•———

Political corruption, and the related action of bribery, refers to crimes committed by state agents (bureaucrats, officials, representatives, etc.) primarily for their own personal, political, material, and nonmaterial gain, "rather than on behalf of a state goal" (Friedrichs, 1995, p. 57). These are generally interpreted as occupational crimes "since they are obviously not intended to promote the government's organizational goals" (Coleman, 1985, p. 87).

Typically, only individual personal gain results from political corruption, although occasionally both state representatives and their organizational unit benefit when this criminal activity is mutually compatible with both personal and organizational goals. Although state workers are typically the recipients of the benefit, private sector representatives provide the incentives (Coleman, 1985, p. 86).

DEFINITIONAL AND CONCEPTUAL ISSUES

Corruption usually includes accepting or soliciting bribes (i.e., usually money or some other economic benefit, like a gift or service). A bribe is something of value (e.g., money, gift, or favor) given or promised to a person who is capable of using his or her position to influence an outcome (*Webster's,* 1996, p. 226). Many observers suggest that corruption should not be considered a political crime, because it most typically involves a personal gain.[1] But if we subscribe to Friedrichs's (1995) perspective, it is definitely a governmental crime: The citizenry's trust has been violated.

Corruption by state officials mainly takes the form of misuses of political power, and mostly for economic gain (Friedrichs, 1995, p. 62). Politician crime is corruption that is committed by individuals for their own political gain. An example of such a crime would be former U.S. President Richard Nixon's alleged theft through his "Plumbers" of Democratic Party papers during the Watergate break-in, in an effort to ensure his reelection (Haldeman, 1994; Woodward & Bernstein, 1974). This concept is generally reserved for only those people who violate laws for their own partisan gain rather than for financial benefit to themselves or an organization. Political corruption is typically personal, but the rewards are partisan rather than immediately pecuniary like taking a bribe (Friedrichs, 1995, p. 73).

THE SPECIAL CASE OF HIGH CRIMES AND MISDEMEANORS

Closely related to corruption is the notion of high crimes and misdemeanors. Recently, perhaps because of the highly visible impeachment proceedings against former President Bill Clinton, students may have heard the term "high crimes and misdemeanors." Traditionally (in England), this charge was used to label severe crimes against the state by someone in a position of higher office. It includes such acts as misappropriation of public funds, interfering in elections, accepting bribes, neglect of duty, and various forms of corruption.

HOW WIDESPREAD IS THE PROBLEM?

Like "run-of-the-mill" property crimes, political corruption often goes undetected and is veiled by the ongoing daily operations of the officeholder (Sykes, 1980, pp. 58-62). Corruption is not necessarily part of a policy, but is embedded in the way a bureaucratic system functions. Undoubtedly, the amount of corruption varies over history, through the course of different administrations and with different government agencies, and is based on the type of political system in operation. It is generally believed and empirically demonstrated that in democracies, with well-developed anticorruption statutes (Green, 1990, p. 166, Transparency International "Corruption Perceptions Index"),[2] corruption is less of a problem. Thus, in many advanced industrialized countries, when corruption is discovered by the media or some watchdog organization like Congress Watch, the Center for Public Integrity, or Transparency International, it has the potential to become a scandal.

HISTORICAL PERSPECTIVE

Bribery and corruption both have long histories. Because of their unique positions and poor remuneration, the first state officials had something to exchange that others, who were not in their positions, did not possess. In fact, bribe taking by public officials has been documented over the past four millennia (Noonan, 1984). Estimates of today's dollar amount of bribe money passed to both public and private officials in the United States, for example, range from $3 billion to $15 billion annually (Coleman, 1995, p. 254).

THE EFFECT OF POLITICAL CORRUPTION

Political corruption is a betrayal of the public trust, and thus the citizenry is the ultimate victim of this political crime. This leads the public to become increasingly cynical and apathetic about politics, politicians, and their deeds and misdeeds (Greider, 1992). Political corruption contributes to far-reaching social harms as the public is deceived, lied to, and in some cases denied the impartial representation due them by state officials. It can also lead to increased scrutiny of public officials, making their jobs more burdensome.

The most serious harms resulting from corruption are symbolic. In advanced industrialized democracies the citizenry increasingly views elected and appointed officials skeptically and cynically. Politicians have been accused of participating in political corruption, resulting in a loss of faith in public institutions and elected and appointed officials that is manifested in declining numbers of voters, growing political apathy, and distrust of public officials (Nye, Zelikow, & King, 1997).

Social harms also result from political corruption and have consequences that are sometimes more far-reaching than the garden-variety crimes generally detailed by the mass media, opposition politicians, and watchdog agencies. Wealthy public officials accused of political corruption enjoy the benefit of the doubt and usually have the resources to buy the best legal representation available. Their resources far exceed those provided to nearly everyone charged with street crimes. Because of access and the broad use of favors, powerful public figures have the ability to slow down the wheels of justice as investigations, hearings, depositions, and trials are delayed at seemingly every turn (Parenti, 1995, chap. 8; Reiman, 1998). Such perceptions of lawmakers are widespread and contribute to ongoing public skepticism regarding their ethics (Greider, 1992).

WHO ARE THE PERPETRATORS?

A multitude of government officials and agents at all levels of government (local, state, and federal) engage in political corruption, including but not limited to elected politicians, appointed officials, judges, police officers, and regulatory agency inspectors.

SINGLING OUT THE DOMINANT TYPES

Two broad types of political corruption—that specific to the legislative process and that connected to law enforcement—are arguably the most important manifestations of this form of state crime.[3] These actions occur "through a person's exercise of state authority . . . [meaning] powers lawfully vested in persons by a state through which those persons can make or enforce laws or command others" (Green, 1990, p. 149). Individuals who have the opportunity to commit such crimes have particular powers with which they can "represent the force of state law in certain decisions" (Green, 1990, p. 149). These two forms of political corruption are the focus of this chapter.

Corruption by Lawmakers

Political corruption in the legislative process is usually in the form of bribe taking. This involves the acceptance of money by public employees in exchange for their using authority and influence in the business of the state (Green, 1990, p. 165). Even though bribe taking as a form of political corruption involves various state occupations and professions, the two most frequent participants in the taking of bribes are legislators and the police, due largely to the frequency and nature of their contacts with the public.

Political corruption among elected and appointed officials is almost always manifested in bribe taking, which includes receiving money and favors in return for supporting or frustrating legislation to benefit the person or organization offering the bribe. And, between the two perpetrators, bribes accepted or solicited by government officials are far more consequential in the long run (Coleman, 1995, p. 255) as this "diffuses its harm throughout an entire populace" (Green, 1990, p. 165).

Laws against bribe taking by members of the U.S. Congress have existed since 1852; the first conviction for such unlawful behavior did not occur until the 20th century. As recently as 1970, "only ten members of Congress had been convicted of crimes involving bribery" (Green, 1990, p. 172). Fortunately for the public, and according to Barlow and Kauzlarich (2002), "In the course of their political careers, government officials sometimes find their past catching up with them after they have moved to national prominence. Such was the case with former Vice President Spiro Agnew and former Labor Secretary Raymond Donovan" (p. 126).

Perhaps the best-known recent incident of congressmen accepting bribes is the 1978 ABSCAM case where they were unknowingly filmed while accepting bribes from FBI undercover agents. Federal agents posed as wealthy Arab businessmen desiring political and business favors from congressional members in exchange for bribes, some of which were as high as $100,000. In all, five congressmen were convicted and sentenced to prison terms ranging from 18 months to 3 years. Not only have federal politicians been indicted and convicted of corruption charges, but so have state and local officials. In addition to ABSCAM, some of the more prominent investigations include the FBI's Greylord Operation, Operation Lost Trout (also known as Bubba Gate), and Azcam (in Arizona) (Sykes & Cullen, 1992, p. 269).

In Canada, over the past two decades, there have been a number of similar cases. One was called the Sky Shops Affair and involved the participation of prominent businessmen and a senator:

> Gordon Brown and Clarence Campbell . . . offered $95,000 to Liberal Senator Lousi Giguere in exchange for his assistance in reversing the federal transport ministry decision not to extend Sky Shop Export Limited's lease to operate a duty-free shop at the government-owned Dorval Airport in

Montreal. . . . Conspiracy charges were subsequently brought against the [participants] . . . Although Brown and Campbell were charged and convicted, Giguere was unexpectedly adjudicated not guilty of conspiring to accept a benefit. (Corrado & Davies, 2000, pp. 63–64)

The acceptance of bribes by lawmakers may be less common than the more subtle forms of influence peddling (e.g., campaign contributions and lobbyists' perks), but it is "the offense that is most likely to lead to the criminal prosecution of elected officials" (Coleman, 1994, p. 50). For example, about 42% of criminal indictments of members of Congress have been for accepting some type of bribe. The most sought-after favors in return for a bribe are the introduction of special bills and the casting of votes in a way that benefits the person offering the bribe. About 30% of charges filed against members of Congress have been for such violations of public trust. In addition, about 27% of indictments have been for helping private business win government contracts (Coleman, 1994, p. 50).

In Canada it is routinely believed that political corruption is rampant in the maritime provinces of Newfoundland, Nova Scotia, and New Brunswick. One of the most colorful episodes concerned former New Brunswick Premier Richard Hatfield, who "rose to prominence in 1970, largely on a platform that emphasized honest government untainted by the corruption that had characterized previous administrations," but who supposedly

received special considerations during a police investigation and his subsequent trial on a criminal drug charge relating to the possession of a small amount of marijuana. Hatfield was acquitted at the end of a very strange trial wherein the trial judge, a Hatfield appointee, accused the journalist of having planted the substantive evidence in Hatfield's luggage. (Corrado & Davies, 2000, p. 65)

Finally, during the mid-1980s, in the Progressive Conservative government of Prime Minister Brian Mulroney, numerous "instances of Tory indiscretion" were brought to public attention, "including objectionable spending habits, blatant patronage and more widespread and insidious scandals." Mulroney's personal disregard for public funds was perhaps best exemplified by a $300,000 "loan" that he secured in 1987 from the PC Canada fund for custom renovations to his official residence (Corrado & Davies, 2000, p. 66).

In 1989, as a result of a perhaps more complicated corruption, Oliver North, a Marine Corps colonel and a national security advisor to then President Ronald Reagan, received public attention because of his activities that were later called the Iran-Contra Scandal (Woodward, 1987). In sum, North was responsible for managing and (depending on which source you believe) orchestrating a deal whereby Nicaraguan Contras were provided financial aid and allowed to secretly sell and/or transport illegal drugs secretly, the profits from which were channeled to Israel to pay for anti-aircraft missiles to be shipped later to Iran. During this time, the congressionally mandated Boland Amendment placed an embargo on not only the types of aid that the Contras could receive, but on the goods the West could supply to Iran. North was charged with lying under oath, obstructing a congressional inquiry, taking money and not claiming it, and destroying government documents. He had also accepted an illegal gratuity—a home security system worth $13,800 (Marshall, Scott, & Hunter, 1987; Woodward, 1987). He was convicted in 1989, but the conviction was overturned because his testimony at the trial had been "immunized." This outcome was predictable because the appellate panel was mostly Republican appointees. Similar outcomes befell North's accomplices Robert McFarlane, Richard R. Miller, and Carl (Spitz) Channel (Shank, 1980, pp. iii-iv).

Corruption by Law Enforcement Officers

Police corruption involves both police and occupational deviance. *Police deviance* has been defined as "activities which are inconsistent with the officer's legal authority, organizational authority, and standards of ethical conduct" (Roberg & Kuykendall, 1993, p. 186). Police corruption is typically not violent, although in some cases the threat or use of force is fundamental to corruption. Police corruption is treated as a form of political crime because it "involves overt criminal activity by police officers" (Roberg & Kuykendall, 1993, p. 190) in the course of their legitimate occupations and is made possible by the legitimate authority of their political occupations (e.g., Green, 1990, chap. 5). Police corruption is conducted for the officer's personal gain and "the use of police power and authority to further that gain" (Kappeler, Sluder, & Alpert, 1994, p. 24). Police corruption is best understood in the context of officers' individual careers, cultures, and socialization into a policeman's personality (e.g., Manning, 1991; Sherman, 1978; Van Maanen, 1973).

Even though the level of police corruption is unknown, there is a nearly universal assumption that it is widespread. Since the establishment of the very first police agency, numerous police departments in advanced industrialized countries have been investigated for corruption. Officers in many big-city police departments in the United States have been investigated for and convicted of having participated in indiscriminate bribe taking. The New York City Police Department (NYPD), for example, has been subjected to at least nine major corruption investigations. The Knapp Commission, which operated between 1967 and 1972, was one of the most publicized corruption investigations in the nation's history. It resulted from the testimony of former NYPD officer Frank Serpico, who alleged that widespread corruption existed among his fellow officers and that senior police administrators knew that this abuse of power was taking place but failed to take appropriate actions to stop it. The Knapp Commission revealed that police corruption took many forms, ranging from the rather innocuous to very serious and lucrative extortion (Maas, 1973).

Corruption like that found in the NYPD in the late 1960s and early 1970s typically included "pads," which are regularly scheduled payoffs, and "scores," which are one-time bribes solicited by the officer or offered to him or her for not enforcing the law. Police corruption also included "Christmas tips," money that is extorted from business establishments and paid to individual officers (Maas, 1973).

During 1994, the NYPD was investigated again by the Mollen Commission as officers revealed that despite a number of controls implemented in the wake of Knapp, corruption similar to that found by the Knapp Commission continued unabated (Kappeler et al., 1994). Furthermore, the bribery was even more lucrative than before, primarily because it involved illegal drug dealing. Investigations of the Chicago and Philadelphia police departments arrived at the same conclusion—that corruption in police ranks was "a widespread and serious problem" (Coleman, 1994, p. 45).

Corruption in law enforcement is more unusual in Canada. Canadian police, whose salaries are regarded as paltry, must investigate drug-related activities where enormous sums of money are generated and exchanged. Bribe taking and corruption are likely, given the complexities of such social phenomena. The police in Canada have engaged in crime for profit by selling immunity and often have committed further crimes to shield their corrupt activities (Forcese, 1992, chap. 5).

Corruption in law enforcement is typically explained as resulting from (a) opportunities available to the police, (b) the buying and selling of vice and the laws designed to control such, and (c) the complexities and subtle nuances of local ordinances. Each of these poses problems for those enforcing laws and each is central to understanding the pervasiveness of corruption among law enforcement officials.

First, those who work in law enforcement (and to some extent in regulatory agencies) have the ability and opportunity to sell immunity from the law (Coleman, 1994, p. 44). As with most traditional forms of corruption, an officer's ability to engage in bribe taking and its relative lucrativeness depend on his or her occupationally bounded opportunities: "an officer assigned to guard City Hall, for instance, ha[s] less opportunity to exercise authority for a bribe than, say, an officer who patrol[s] an area where prostitution, drugs, and gambling [are] rampant" (Green, 1990, p. 170). As street-level bureaucrats, police officers have opportunities available to them in their everyday work settings, especially given their autonomy because they work either alone or in pairs with minimal direct supervision. The sheer numbers of people who desire the services and discretion that police have at their disposal, and who have little regard for the laws that constrict their material and nonmaterial betterment, also contribute to police officers' propensity for corruption (Coleman, 1994, p. 45).

Second, vice laws, which prohibit and criminalize goods and services that countless millions of consumers demand, are themselves criminogenic in that they create environments fostering corruption and bribery. Prostitution, gambling, and the sale of illegal drugs are profitable industries that, to some extent, are by necessity conducted in the open. Participants in vice transactions have some level of immunity; otherwise, they could not continue conducting business in the highly visible nature that vice demands. In other words, police do not make arrests every time they witness the buying or selling of vice.

Corruption by Regulatory Inspectors

Local ordinances, often complex and voluminous, particularly in the case of regulatory laws, allow law enforcement agents ample opportunity for discriminately deciding just how to proceed with violations. Building ordinances, laws governing surface coal mining, and local fire codes, for example, are often too numerous and dynamic for builders, mine operators, and night club managers, among others, to obey. By simply doing business, they more than likely are in violation of some local ordinance. As a result, they willingly abide by the more serious laws and often pay off police officers and regulatory inspectors for ignoring many other typically less serious violations. Some building contractors and construction companies are happy to pay off inspectors, believing that bribes are much less costly than abiding by the letter of the law (Coleman, 1994). These particular forms of political corruption are considered occupational crimes because they are not intended to benefit or promote a government's organizational goals (Coleman, 1994, p. 45).

Regulatory inspectors who are responsible for ensuring workers' and consumers' safety have been known to accept bribes for instrumental rather than organizational agendas. They accept bribes in exchange for looking the other way; falsifying governmental reports regarding work-site conditions; and issuing citations for minor infractions rather than major, perhaps life-threatening violations of law.

But, from the evidence available, it appears that bribery and other forms of corruption are not nearly as prevalent among regulatory inspectors as they are among police officers (Coleman, 1994). Several factors may account for these differences. First, unlike police departments, regulatory agencies typically do not have generations-old cultures of corruption into which individual employees are socialized. Second, law enforcement officers working in vice are presented with numerous opportunities to accept bribes and can rationalize their unwillingness to enforce the law with the belief that no one is being harmed because vice participants almost always voluntarily participate in their vice. This supplies the rationale and notion of "victimless crimes." For this reason, it is safe to assume that regulatory inspectors responsible for the safety of workers and consumers cannot rationalize their unwillingness to enforce the law as easily as, say, vice patrol officers. Third, regulatory inspectors do not deal on a daily basis with actively known violators of the law, unlike, for example, vice officers. As a result, regulatory inspectors are exposed to far fewer opportunities and are approached by individuals willing to bribe them far less often than police officers on the street. Yet because they monitor the more lucrative forms of deviance, such as white-collar crimes, regulatory inspectors who choose to accept bribes have the opportunity to pocket far greater sums of money from a single bribe than most street police officers.

SUMMARY

Politicians, police officers, and regulatory inspectors do not necessarily resemble criminals on the surface, yet it is well known that some of them engage in a number of crimes, including political corruption. Political corruption remains a fundamental problem for advanced industrialized democracies. Within the cultures of politics and policing there remains a veil of secrecy and a distrust of outsiders. In some cases, violating laws is fundamental to the occupational cultural norms and values of politics and policing. Thus, quite often both the public and the state expect these activities to go hand in hand.

NOTES

1. A similar response is given regarding smuggling. Over history, countries have embargoed the sales of particular things, especially military weapons, to those states they believe are national security risks. Since the 1970s this has happened with increasing frequency against individuals supplying Libya, Iran, and Iraq with weaponry.

2. Since 1995, Transparency International (TI) has conducted an annual "Corruptions Perceptions Index" that ranks 90 countries "in terms of the degree to which corruption is perceived to exist among public officials and politicians." It appears each year that the advanced industrialized countries are the least corrupt.

3. During the Reagan administration, the Justice Department, under the direction of Attorney General Ed Meese, allegedly stole software from a company called INSLAW and tried to force the company out of business and give this product to friends of the Regan administration (Fricker & Pizzo, 1992).

TEST QUESTIONS

Multiple-Choice

1. What was the name of the commission that investigated corruption in the NYPD because of Serpico's testimony?
   a. Mollen
   b. Reiman
   c. Knapp
   d. Sykes
   e. all of the above

2. What is corruption that is committed by individuals for their own political gain?
   a. state crimes
   b. sedition
   c. all crimes
   d. politician crime
   e. none of the above

3. Between which years did the Knapp Commission operate?
   a. 1967-1972
   b. 1954-1964
   c. 1980-1987
   d. 2000-2001
   e. all of the above

4. When was the first conviction of a member of the U.S. Congress for bribe taking?
   a. 1890
   b. 1900
   c. 1952
   d. 20th century
   e. none of the above

5. For which of the following occupations do we know the least about political corruption?
   a. regulatory inspectors
   b. police officers
   c. politicians
   d. all of the above
   e. none of the above

6. In which country did the Sky Shops affair take place?
   a. United States
   b. Canada
   c. Great Britain
   d. France
   e. Australia

7. Who was the decorated U.S. Marine officer who was implicated in the Iran-Contra affair?
   a. G. Gordon Liddy
   b. George Bush
   c. Richard Milhous Nixon
   d. James Trafficant
   e. Oliver North

Short Answers

1. What are three reasons why corruption exists in law enforcement?

2. Why do some scholars and observers believe that corruption is not really a political crime? Do you agree with them?

3. What is a high crime and misdemeanor?

4. How widespread is political corruption?

EIGHT

ILLEGAL DOMESTIC SURVEILLANCE

D omestic surveillance consists of a variety of information-gathering activities conducted primarily by the state's coercive agencies (i.e., police, national security, and military). These actions are conducted against citizens, organizations, businesses, and foreign governments. Such operations usually include opening mail, listening to telephone conversations (i.e., eavesdropping and wiretapping), reading electronic communications, and infiltrating groups (whether they be legal, illegal, or deviant). Although a legitimate law enforcement technique, surveillance is often considered unpalatable to the public in general and civil libertarians in particular. This is especially true when state agents cross the line and conduct searches without warrants, collect evidence that is beyond the scope of the warrant, or harass and destabilize their targets.[1] These latter activities are illegal (because of the Constitution, statutes, regulations, and ordinances that specify the conditions under which surveillance may be conducted) and are the focus of this chapter, which concentrates on illegal domestic rather than foreign surveillance.[2] Here we must also be cautious about distinguishing between spying or espionage, which is conducted against a foreign government, and illegal domestic surveillance.

DEFINITIONAL AND CONCEPTUAL ISSUES

Although it is recognized that domestic surveillance is crucial for particular types of legitimate law enforcement campaigns, and is often a useful information-gathering tactic, state agencies and employees repeatedly spy on individuals and groups in an illegal fashion. This unlawful activity takes place largely because state agents have defined the target's political ideologies, affiliations, and strategies as being deviant.

The majority of intelligence is collected from open sources (i.e., available to the general public). Skilled intelligence/national security officers are very adept at using publicly available data sources to obtain the kinds of information they need to do their job. In most cases there is no need to use a surreptitious listening device (or "bug," as it is colloquially referred to). Generally, good intelligence officers are often better at finding information than seasoned reference librarians. Intelligence personnel also have the option of using human sources. It is not illegal to observe or ask people questions, and it is not necessary to have a warrant to carry on an information-probing conversation. Then again, those questioned by an intelligence officer are not under any legal obligation to speak or to tell the truth. If they do fabricate information, however, they may later be charged with impeding an investigation.

HOW WIDESPREAD IS THE PROBLEM?

Even though the intensity and pervasiveness of a nation's surveillance of its citizens waxes and wanes over time, it is the stock-in-trade of domestic law enforcement (Marx, 1988). Domestic surveillance has been a part of law enforcement since the birth of policing, although it has become much more widespread since the 1930s and has been used against a greater number of people defined as threats to "national order," dissident groups, labor unions, and political activists (e.g., Coleman, 1985, chap. 2; Harring, 1983; Quinney, 1974, chap. 4; Theoharis, 1978; Tunnell, 1995a, 1995b).

CAUSES

The most telling factor for understanding who is labeled threatening and who is not resides in the concept of the maintenance of power. Because of the inordinate resource differentials between the state and dissidents, governments, through various channels of communication and networks, can easily label groups or individuals as criminal or as threats to national security. Compared to private entities, the state can more easily justify its actions as necessary and persuade the public to believe that groups such as Students for a Democratic Society (SDS; an organization in the United States committed to advancing civil rights and ending the war in Vietnam) or Parti Québécois (PQ; a Canadian group that wanted the province of Québec to separate from the rest of Canada) are inappropriate, extreme, radical, subversive, or armed terrorists capable of destabilizing "our democratic way of life." Moreover, it is very difficult for these organizations to demonstrate successfully to the public and the media that governments and their agents also violate the law.

Although the state typically has a legitimate monopoly on force and law, it tends to rely on repressive surveillance mainly during crises (Torrance, 1977, 1995). This was evident in the United States, for example, during the political disturbances of the 1960s and 1970s when SDS and the Black Panther Party (BPP) were politically active, and again during the 1980s when critical questions were raised regarding U.S. policies toward Central America. Not only did the FBI place the SDS under surveillance, but local municipal police departments also spied on them (Churchill & Vander Wall, 1988). The FBI determined that the group's activities were threatening to the status quo and that the SDS ideology embraced communism. Soon, every FBI field office in the country became involved in the ongoing surveillance of the SDS (Donner, 1990). Although the political Right has been and is today spied on primarily due to officials' perceptions that they are well armed and potentially violent, historically it is the Left that regularly has been victim to domestic surveillance operations (Coleman, 1995, p. 258; Zwerman, 1989). Today's criminal investigations into the September 11, 2001, attacks on the World Trade Center and the Pentagon more than likely will be interpreted by historians and other analysts as an instance of unnecessary surveillance.

Little consensus exists in the public on the legality and necessity of domestic surveillance. The organizational mind-set of law enforcement agencies, national security agencies, and the military supports the use of domestic surveillance as essential for protecting national security, preventing disruptions of social order, and in some instances maintaining capitalism, power, and privilege as the dominant economic order.

THE EFFECT OF ILLEGAL DOMESTIC SURVEILLANCE

Through domestic surveillance it is possible to gather useful information to combat oppositional political crime. Many people, however, are opposed to this state activity because they value their right to privacy and because domestic surveillance tests constitutional guarantees and civil rights. In addition, the public believes that government agencies have no right to spy on citizens except under the most unusual circumstances. This is why previous domestic spying operations have come under fire by opponents who claim that a government's spying on its citizens is criminal.

Domestic surveillance has wide-ranging implications, particularly if an individual is innocent, because damage or harm may be done to his or her reputation and employability (Churchill & Vander Wall, 1988). For example, during the 1950s, many individuals who were falsely accused by the McCarthy Commission suffered considerable psychological and financial damage (Navansky, 1991). Some, due to either economic reasons or disgust, left the United States.

Such illegal surveillance and the corresponding possibilities for misuse of increasingly sophisticated surveillance technologies available in the contemporary information age are the "negative features" of law enforcement surveillance (Marx, 1988, p. 222). The sheer number of new tools available to agents in the crime control industry (Christie, 1993) is disturbing, as they are extended to and used against people and organizations who are not involved in or suspected of committing crimes, but rather are defined as potentially threatening to the dominant political and economic order.

Increasingly, intelligence agencies are moving from human sources (i.e., HUMINT) to signals intelligence (i.e., SIGINT) and other types of intelligence (Laqueur, 1985). Intelligence agencies are able to keep up with changes in technology that political criminals may have. Echelon, as mentioned before, is a case in point.

State agencies in democratic countries typically spy because individuals and groups come to be defined as security risks or threats to national order. Whether they are or are not actual threats often is irrelevant; the telling characteristic is that they are *defined* as such by those with the power and authority to set in motion the state's surveillance machinery.

Undoubtedly, some constituencies (e.g., governmental agents and apologists) explain away such activities as anomalies or the actions of a few deviant or rogue governmental employees. But many domestic surveillance operations were simply too complex, involved too many state agents and offices, and were either directed by or had the blessings of top-level administrators to have resulted from a few misguided, front-line employees. These activities were organizational in nature, meaning that the spy programs became standard operating procedure for certain government agencies (Coleman, 1985, chap. 2).

HISTORICAL PERSPECTIVE

Federal and local law enforcement in all three countries featured in this book have periodically engaged in illegal domestic surveillance.

A multitude of government intelligence agencies operate in the United States. They include the CIA, the FBI, the National Reconnaissance Office, the National Security Agency, the Defense Intelligence Agency, the State Department Bureau of Intelligence and Research, the Drug Enforcement Agency, and a number of Pentagon organizations. The FBI and the CIA, in particular, are the most well-known government organizations for which we have the most evidence of illegal domestic surveillance operations (Ranelagh, 1987). In Canada, the former Royal Canadian Mounted Police-Security Service (RCMP-SS) and the Canadian Security Intelligence Service (CSIS) have played similar questionable roles (Brown & Brown, 1978; Dion, 1982; Sawatsky, 1980). And in the United Kingdom, surveillance and other questionable techniques are usually carried out by MI-5 or MI-6. The FBI and RCMP are national police forces with the responsibility for policing domestically (although FBI field offices now exist in several countries, including the former "nemesis," Russia, and the RCMP has officers in many embassies throughout the world). The CIA, on the other hand, concentrates its activities abroad. And although many Americans disagree with its operations, such work is largely accepted as necessary for "national security."

Research on these agencies has been produced by reporters and scholars, and as the result of government inquiries. This takes place at the national and local levels. It is often supported by organizations like the Canadian Association for Security and Intelligence Studies (CASIS) or the "Intelligence Section" of the International Studies Association (ISA).

The American Experience

One of the most widely used spying techniques is wiretapping, declared illegal in the United States in 1934. Although the FBI continued using this technology as it had before, agents did discontinue its use briefly after a 1937 Supreme Court ruling that applied the law to the FBI and its operations. Two years later, President Franklin Roosevelt claimed the FBI had the authority and right to wiretap in "national security" cases (Coleman, 1985, p. 59). Wiretapping remained illegal until 1968 when it was ruled permissible if authorized by court order based on sufficient probable cause. Despite this judicial intervention, illegal domestic surveillance continued unabated. Also, criminal justice personnel often have to go "judge shopping" in order to gain the trust or confidence of a sympathetic judge. Illegally planting listening devices, or bugs, is possible mainly through burglaries. Though the rate of using these devices has varied, former FBI Director J. Edgar Hoover continued condoning illegal burglaries and the planting of bugs (Coleman, 1985, p. 60).

Even though a federal court order is necessary for any law enforcement agency to open private mail, between 1959 and 1966 the FBI examined 42 million pieces of mail in New York City alone. Furthermore, the CIA, prohibited by legislation from engaging in domestic surveillance, read private mail sent to and from the United States and the former USSR during the height of the Cold War. It has been determined that they opened 216,000 pieces of mail and compiled a list of 1.5 million names of individuals from these mailings alone (CIA's Mail Intercept, 1975; Coleman, 1985; Halperin, Burosage, & Marwick, 1977).

The FBI and the CIA are not the only agencies that have been accused of illegal domestic surveillance. Although he denied it, former President Richard Nixon assembled the "Plumbers," "an investigation team organized under the aegis of the President and his staff" engaged in political sabotage. Formed in 1971, they apparently "coordinated the congressional investigations into the leaking of the Pentagon Papers. . . . The administration hoped to secure prosecution of the individual who released the papers on grounds of espionage" (Roebuck & Weeber, 1978, p. 23).

In 1972, the Plumbers also burglarized and bugged the Democratic National Committee's (DNC) headquarters, located in the Watergate Building in Washington, D.C., in an attempt to steal secret DNC materials (Haldeman, 1994; Woodward & Bernstein, 1974). When investigations into the Plumbers were conducted, it was found that they "ultimately handled such tasks as forging diplomatic cables and hiring thugs to disrupt peace rallies" (Roebuck & Weeber, 1978, p. 24).

Another important instance of illegal surveillance took place during the Iran-Contra conspiracy in which U.S. government agents, under the direction of Lt. Colonel Oliver North, sold arms to Iran (Woodward, 1987). These actions violated U.S. policies "against arming Iran and dealing for hostages, marking up the price of the arms and selling the profit to the Nicaraguan contras in violation of the congressional Boland Amendment forbidding aid" (Williams, 1991, p. 12).

Even though dissident groups in the United States had suspected for some time that they were being spied on, infiltrated, and to some extent destabilized by the FBI, it was not until March 8, 1971, that their suspicions were confirmed. On that date a group identifying itself as the Citizens' Commission burgled a regional FBI office in Media, Pennsylvania (Davis, 1992, chap. 1). The Citizens' Commission stole about one thousand Counter-Intelligence Program (COINTELPRO) documents that indicated that for years the FBI had operated a national, organizational, and illegal surveillance operation against several dissident groups in America. The spying focused primarily on the New Left, which is composed of disparate but like-minded groups. FBI files also revealed that the BPP, the American Indian Movement (AIM), SDS, and the Communist Party of the United States. (CPUSA) had all been extensively spied on, infiltrated, and had their activities disrupted (Blackstock, 1975; Churchill & Vander Wall, 1990, chap. 7; Davis, 1992, chap. 6).[3] Later,

> Court records in 1977 revealed that the FBI paid $2.5 million in Chicago to recruit an army of more than 5,000 spies who informed on Chicago-area residents and organizations between 1966 and 1976. During the same period, the FBI opened files on about 27,900 individuals and organizations in Chicago who were regarded as possible security risks or extremists. (Roebuck & Weeber, 1978)

After photocopying the FBI's files, the Citizens' Commission mailed them to various journalists, academics, and members of Congress (Davis, 1992, p. 7). The resulting congressional investigation of the FBI revealed that COINTELPRO was illegal and unconstitutional. Furthermore, it showed that the operation, which had existed since 1956, involved 12 separate counterintelligence programs (each involving a different citizens group); that every one was initiated on Hoover's directives; and that the operation involved every FBI field office in the United States. The FBI and Hoover assured Congress that COINTELPRO and similar domestic surveillance operations were discontinued on April 28, 1971 (Churchill & Vander Wall, 1990). Yet just a few years later another FBI spy program was in place and aimed at the citizens group CISPES.

The FBI's investigation of CISPES began in March 1983 and ultimately involved 52 FBI field offices (Davis, 1992, chap. 7). As in earlier surveillance programs, people were covertly investigated because of their political rather than criminal activities. Also, this spy operation, like earlier COINTELPRO activities, was not the product of "rogue" FBI agents operating without proper authorization. Directives concerning this operation came from FBI headquarters, as was indicated by a March 30, 1983, FBI memo instructing 11 field offices to begin surveillance specifically on individuals involved in CISPES (Davis, 1992, p. 178).

CISPES had developed because many U.S. citizens grew concerned about the continued financial and military support of the El Salvadoran government, a regime that most human rights watch groups considered repressive (Power, 1981, pp. 44-61). Because of its commitment to the government of El Salvador, the United States defined groups opposing its capital and foreign policy toward El Salvador as sympathetic to leftists in Central America and as threatening to ongoing relationships and stability in that region. Thus, CISPES found itself under surveillance; its offices were mysteriously burgled and activities were infiltrated and disrupted by the FBI.

The FBI's operations were uncovered through a search using the Freedom of Information Act. As a response to the adverse publicity this garnered, William Sessions, the new FBI director, ignored the organizational nature of this program and imposed disciplinary sanctions against six agents. Nonetheless, a Senate Select Committee criticized the FBI and its continuing surveillance of people and groups involved in dissident political activities while the FBI had claimed that domestic surveillance had been discontinued.[4]

During the 1960s, the CIA

> investigate[d] and determine[d] whether foreign elements had infiltrated protest activity. This program, Operation CHAOS, involved the surveillance activities of domestic groups and violated the CIA's initial charter, the National Security Act, which clearly excluded its activities from the domestic arenas. (Hagan, 1997, p. 33)

Illegal domestic surveillance has undoubtedly reached into the highest law enforcement and administrative offices. It often has been official yet covert organizational policy; these actions have been standard operating procedure supported by numerous field offices, agents, and headquarters, and have been approved and directed by administrators and, in some cases, presidents.

The Canadian Experience

Canadian citizens also have been subjected to illegal surveillance by their law enforcement communities. The McDonald and Keable Commissions Enquiry (Canada, 1991a, 1991b) revealed that the RCMP Security Service, in particular, has engaged in activities similar to those of the FBI. The RCMP periodically has engaged in surveillance against dissident, labor, and leftist groups and people.[5] For example, during the 1960s, the Agency Presse Libre du Québec (APLQ) and the Movement for the Defense of Political Prisoners of Québec (MDPPQ) were both spied on by the RCMP-SS, sometimes in cooperation with the Montreal Urban Community Police Department (MUCPD) and Sureté (the Québec Police Force) (Sawatsky, 1980). The APLQ and the MDPPQ were perceived to be threatening to Québec's and Canada's social order because, according to law enforcement officials, they had as their goals "to publish political bulletins about events in Québec and to transform society" (Dion, 1982, p. 52). Furthermore, the police described the general ideology and ongoing objectives of the APLQ as expressing "the grievances and the interests of workers and of progressive organizations struggling against the present economic and political system" (Dion, 1982, p. 53). When these groups were defined as threatening to the existing order, programs designed to monitor, contain, sabotage, and destabilize their activists were initiated.

In October 1972, in Montreal, the RCMP-SS, along with the MUCPD and Sureté, burgled the offices of the APLQ. About one ton of documents was stolen—all believed to be relevant to the APLQ's ongoing political agenda to work against the dominant political and economic order (Dion, 1982, chap. 1). This particular crime was not the first for the RCMP, for it had broken into the APLQ offices a year earlier to plant listening devices and had reentered at times to repair them. Eventually the police analyzed, photocopied, hid, and finally destroyed the stolen documents.

The RCMP also investigated alleged homosexuals working for the government. If individuals were found to be gay, they were asked to resign or were fired (Sawatsky, 1980, chap. 10). Similarly, the leftist Partisan Party of

Table 8.1   Countries, National Security/Intelligence Agencies and Well-Known
Acts of Illegal Domestic Surveillance

Country	*Most Prominent National Security/Intelligence Agencies*	*Well-Known Acts of Domestic Surveillance*
United States	Federal Bureau of Investigation Central Intelligence Agency	COINTELPRO CISPES investigation Operation CHAOS
Canada	Royal Canadian Mounted Police–Security Service (now the Canadian Security Intelligence Service)	Numerous actions during the 1960s-1970s against pro-separatist factions
United Kingdom	MI-5 MI-6 Special Branch	Stalker Affair Birmingham Six Guildford Four

Vancouver, later amalgamated into the Canadian Communist Party, was spied
on and had files stolen by the RCMP—these were disruptive rather than intel-
ligence-gathering tactics (Sawatsky, 1980, chap. 20).

The British Experience

The security service and police intelligence agencies of Great Britain
include MI-5, the Secret Intelligence Branch (SIS, or MI-6 as it is commonly
called), Special Branch, and the Anti-Terrorist Branch.[6] According to Thurlow
(1994) there have been "three main targets of political surveillance, the
Communist Party of Great Britain, the British Union of Fascists, and the
Sinn Fein and its links with the Irish Republican Army" (p. 3).

> The most extreme domestic concern was the activities of the IRA and
> its splinter groups, which have been involved in spasmodic guerilla warfare
> with the British state since 1916. . . . The British state saw the IRA as
> political terrorists, while the IRA's self-image was one of freedom fighting.
> (Thurlow, 1994, p. 8)

Stemming from the "Northern Ireland problem," British intelligence
was accused of illegal surveillance in what were later called the Stalker Affair
and the trials of the Birmingham Six and the Guildford Four (Ross, 2000a);
see Table 8.1.

ILLEGAL DOMESTIC SURVEILLANCE
BY LOCAL POLICE FORCES

Historical analyses of the rise of police surveillance beginning in the days of intense labor struggles and violence (e.g., the Haymarket tragedy of May 1886) show that it grew nearly exponentially from the 1930s through the 1960s (Donner, 1990). Most big-city police agencies (e.g., Chicago, New York City, Los Angeles, and Philadelphia) have spied on American citizens (Donner, 1990). Each had special units whose responsibilities were solely information gathering, infiltrating, and destabilizing citizens' groups defined as threatening to the social order (Donner, 1990). While engaging in their own surveillance operations, city police departments often acted in tandem with national law enforcement agencies, most typically the FBI and the RCMP.

For example, the Chicago Police Department's (CPD) political surveillance operation claimed in 1960 that it "had accumulated information on some 117,000 local individuals, 141,000 out-of-town subjects, and 14,000 organizations" (Donner, 1990, p. 92). Until 1968, most of its spying had been limited to ideologically threatening groups—the Communist Party and the Socialist Workers' Party. But with the Democratic National Convention scheduled for Chicago in 1968, surveillance increased and included a wide variety of "civic groups and prominent citizens," linking them, as best the authorities could, to communism and communist subversion, although next to no substantiation ever materialized (Donner, 1990, p. 93). Groups spied on by the CPD included the American Civil Liberties Union (ACLU), the National Association for the Advancement of Colored People (NAACP), People United to Save Humanity, the National Lawyers' Guild, the League of Women Voters, the World Council of Churches, universities, and churches.

Finally, in March of 1975, a Cook County (Chicago) grand jury heard testimony on the intelligence unit within the Chicago Police Department and subsequently issued a report strongly condemning its activities. Intelligence unit officers who were ordered to testify before the grand jury told of the division's illegalities. "In addition to illegal electronic surveillance, police officers admittedly engaged in burglaries, thefts, incitements to violence, destruction of mailing lists, and other criminal acts because 'they believed it their duty'" (Donner, 1990, p. 104).[7] Although allegedly dissolved in 1975, 6 years later the CPD admitted in federal court that since then its intelligence unit had kept files for surveillance-related purposes on 77 civic, religious, antiwar, civil rights, and political organizations, ranging from the Chicago Parent-Teacher Association to an assortment of church groups, raising to at least 800 the total number of such files. . . . Moreover, individual dossiers were recorded in thousands of files and on tens of thousands of index cards. (Donner, 1990, p. 153)

New York City had its own spy unit, the Bureau of Special Services (BOSS), and Philadelphia, under former mayor Frank Rizzo, the son of a police sergeant and a career police officer himself, established its own surveillance unit known as the Civil Defense Squad. The New York, Philadelphia, and later the Los Angeles Police Departments operated similarly to the surveillance squad of Chicago—clearly violating laws and spying on their cities' own citizens. Each department now claims its spy operations defunct, although just after former Los Angeles police chief Daryl Gates retired in 1993, evidence emerged indicating that he had used a special LAPD surveillance force for spying on various leftist sympathizers and political enemies, including the actor Robert Redford and former mayor Tom Bradley (Rothmiller & Goldman, 1992). We can only speculate about whether these surveillance units are truly things of the past. If history is any judge, that seems doubtful.

SUMMARY

This chapter illustrates that illegal domestic surveillance is not an isolated phenomenon. Rather, it has been an ongoing organizational policy and practice in democratic states and, in some cases, has been sanctioned by heads of state. Furthermore, surveillance operations have been launched against both violators of the criminal law and individuals involved in legal political dissident.

Critical questions are raised regarding domestic surveillance as political crime. For example, at what point is spying elevated to an illegitimate form of political policing to become criminal? And how is politics or political ideology relevant to a government's surveillance of its own citizens? These questions are fundamentally important for understanding the subtle nuances of the illegal spying that threatens the legal and constitutional guarantees enjoyed by citizens of democracies. And, as Sykes (1980, pp. 57-58) has made clear about the U.S. experience with domestic surveillance and other political crimes of the state, these crimes may be the dirty work that people abhor but nonetheless consider necessary. Given the history of illegal domestic surveillance in industrialized democracies, it is reasonable to expect such programs to continue at some level.

NOTES

1. This kind of action violates generally accepted standards of civil rights. In the United States, in particular, the Constitution, through the Fourth Amendment, guarantees everyone to be safe from unreasonable searches of their homes.

2. Foreign surveillance was treated earlier (Chapter 4), in the previous discussion on espionage.

3. Immediately after the break-in, then-FBI Director Herbert Hoover closed 100 of the FBI's offices and ordered in 100 special agents with a single objective—find the Citizens' Commission. The group was never located, and the case remains unsolved today (Davis, 1992).

4. Beyond this condemnation from the Senate Committee, in a federal lawsuit, the Socialist Workers Party was awarded damages resulting from the FBI's ongoing surveillance, infiltration, and disruption of their political activities. It was discovered that between 1960 and 1966 the FBI had burglarized the Socialist Workers Party's offices at least 94 times, an average of once every 3 weeks for 6½ years, to photograph and steal various documents (Coleman, 1985; Davis, 1992).

5. The RCMP Security Service has been replaced by the Canadian Security Intelligence Service.

6. For an in-depth review of domestic intelligence in Great Britain see, for example, Bunyan (1976).

7. The grand jury concluded that primary surveillance targets were almost entirely groups opposing Chicago's former Mayor Richard Daley and his policies. Furthermore, they stated that "groups which received the most intensive scrutiny had also been openly critical of some policies of the Chicago Police Department" (Donner, 1990, p. 104).

TEST QUESTIONS

Multiple-Choice

1. What is the name given to the group that burglarized and bugged the Democratic National Committee Headquarters in 1972?
   a. the Electricians
   b. the Plumbers
   c. the Stockers
   d. the Painters
   e. the Engineers

2. In October 1972, in Montreal, who burglarized the offices of the APLQ?
   a. RCMP-SS
   b. MUCPD
   c. NYPD
   d. FBI
   e. both a and b

3. Where was the Bureau of Special Services located?
   a. California
   b. Oregon
   c. Maine
   d. New York
   e. Maryland

4. The majority of intelligence gathered by national security agencies is collected from
   a. closed sources
   b. open sources
   c. interviews
   d. questionnaires
   e. all of the above

5. Domestic surveillance is primarily conducted by
   a. police
   b. national security agencies
   c. military
   d. all of the above
   e. none of the above

6. In the United States, in order for wiretapping to be legal, what do national security/intelligence agencies need?
   a. proper training
   b. court order
   c. to be accompanied by a police officer
   d. good equipment
   e. all the above

7. What is the name of the FBI operation that conducted surveillance of several dissident groups in the United States, especially those of the New Left?
    a. COINTELPRO
    b. BOSS
    c. CHAOS
    d. ECHELON
    e. none of the above

Short Answer

1. What is the difference between HUMINT and SIGINT?

2. What four illegal operations/activities did the RCMP-SS engage in between the 1950s and the beginning of the McDonald enquiry?

3. List four well-known political whistleblowers.

4. Is there a difference between espionage and illegal domestic surveillance? Why or why not?

❊ NINE ❊

HUMAN RIGHTS VIOLATIONS

———•◦•———

One of the most well publicized and accepted state crimes is human rights violations (Cohen, 1993). With increasing frequency, the media report on human rights violations and recent efforts to bring to justice the individuals and states committing these crimes. For example, as recently as 2001 the British government attempted to deport former Chilean dictator Augusto Pinochet to Spain, and there were rumblings among the Western Left community over the possibility of arresting and trying Henry Kissinger, former U.S. secretary of state during the Nixon era, as a war criminal (e.g., Hitchens, 2001). During the summer of 2001, Slobodan Milosevic, the former president of Yugoslavia, was finally handed over by Serbian authorities to the International Court of Justice in The Hague.

DEFINITIONAL AND CONCEPTUAL ISSUES

Human rights abuses include both violent and nonviolent actions. Examples of the former infringements include committing people to mental hospitals, beating, torturing, executing dissidents, and genocide. Instances of the latter types of actions encompass restrictions on political participation, including disallowing individuals their right to vote for representative government; preventing dissident political activities and organizations; arbitrary detention; restrictions on the freedoms of expression, association, assembly, and religion; violations of due process; discrimination based on racial, gender, ethnic, and religious grounds; and continuing institutionalized sexism and racism.

Regardless of the degree of violence in connection with these actions, human rights violations are usually carried out by or have the involvement of a variety of state criminogenic agencies, including the armed forces, national security agencies, police, and government sponsored militias, the most frightening type being death squads.

It is only recently that such issues have been treated as political crimes by a small yet vocal body of criminologists. Previously, they were simply considered social problems—for example, those beyond people's control, or resulting from the whims of an unpredictable market economy, and in some cases, brought upon individuals by their own deficiencies. Many criminologists and progressive-minded individuals and organizations have interpreted commissive and omissive behaviors of states as human rights abuses (e.g., Cohen, 1993).

Some of these actions include homelessness (e.g., Barak, 1991), poverty, the "grossly inequitable distribution of wealth in the United States," hunger (Bohm, 1993, p. 8), the greatly increasing numbers of prisoners, and the selective incarceration of individual "political prisoners" as violations of basic human rights. Part of the problem with human rights violations is cultural relativism. In other words, some observers suggest that in order to protect state sovereignty, we should not mingle in the affairs of another when we don't understand or cannot appreciate cultural practices that may appear to us as brutal or repressive (e.g., Pollis & Schwab, 1979).

HOW WIDESPREAD IS THE PROBLEM?

The pervasiveness of human rights violations is difficult to determine due to governmental secrecy, the reluctance of victims and perpetrators to come forward, and the unwillingness of repressive governments to make such information accessible. It is also impossible to determine the numbers of political prisoners, although some human rights organizations (e.g., Amnesty International) are considered to have very reliable data. It is clear that although human rights violations are rare occurrences in the Anglo American democracies, they take place at alarming rates throughout the world in countries that have totalitarian or authoritarian regimes. Perhaps more important, many oppressive countries are either supported or tolerated by the Anglo American democracies.

Human Rights Violations in the United States

Incarcerating those who oppose the government is a form of human rights abuse that seemingly pervades states regardless of their political-economic systems. Countries as diverse as Burma and England, China and the United States, and El Salvador and Russia have all selectively imprisoned dissidents.

During the War of 1812, the U.S. government, as a security precaution, arrested numerous British citizens who were living in East Coast cities. During World War I (1914-1918), the United States interned 6,000 German and other European-born civilians in military barracks in Georgia, Tennessee, and Utah. A third, more recent example was during World War II (1941-1945) when 120,000 Japanese American citizens (born in the United States) and 8,000 Japanese aliens were detained in prison camps. To their numbers add 3,500 Germans and 1,000 Italians. The internment included women and children and lasted through the declaration of peace. These innocent people lost their jobs, their homes, and suffered great hardship (Goldstein, 1978).

Recent examples of human rights violations in the United States include the behavior modification "high security units" at the federal penitentiaries in Marion, Illinois, and Lexington, Kentucky, where once politically active individuals were imprisoned until Amnesty International investigated and condemned the ongoing practices of the U.S. Bureau of Prisons (Zwerman, 1988).

Beyond these special units, prisons across the United States house "political prisoners," that is, people who have received very lengthy prison sentences and whose incapacitation is qualitatively different from other inmates because of their once-active political participation (e.g., Deutsch & Susler, 1991; Ross & Richards, 2002). Furthermore, the U.S. government, through the attorney general's office and the Immigration and Naturalization Service, violated the human rights of many of the Mariel Cubans who immigrated to the United States in 1980 and quickly found themselves imprisoned in maximum security facilities without having been accused of committing crimes, without trials, and without any due process proceedings (Hamm, 1995).

The United States often finds itself out of step with the world community and indifferent to decisions of the World Court when that court's opinions and rulings are incongruous with U.S. interests (e.g., Robertson, 2000). For example, in the late 1980s America found it convenient to ignore allegations by the World Court that it was in violation of international law in its mining of Managua's harbor in Nicaragua. Barak (1993) offers further critical words about the role of the United States in recent history:

> For the past two decades, of all governments in the West, it has been the United States that has most consistently opposed the realization of the right of self-determinism by the peoples of developing nations. . . . When it has come to the ratification of the major multi-lateral human rights agreements or instruments, the United States has one of the very worst records among Western liberal democracies. By refusing to sign and recognize these various documents, the United States has, at least indirectly, contributed to the worldwide abuse of human rights. (p. 220)

Difficulties in addressing such state human rights abuses rest centrally on the dual role of the state; in these and other cases of human rights abuses the state is both violator and adjudicator.

Human Rights Violations in Great Britain

The detention of citizens and the use of highly questionable interrogation methods, including allegations of torture, by the British Army in Northern Ireland have led to several human rights complaints and official investigations (Ross, 2000a). In 1971, for example, the British army detained and interrogated 14 alleged members of the Irish Republican Army (IRA) Provisionals, using a number of questionable interrogation techniques and sensory deprivation such as "prolonged wall standing, loud noises, hooding, and deprivation of food, water, and sleep" (Roberts, 1976, p. 16; see also Hurwitz, 1995, p. 301).

Consequently, that same year, the neighboring Republic of Ireland sent a petition of complaint to the European Court of Human Rights. "Although the Irish petition contained a series of charges and demands, the most important and significant component of the Irish petition was the allegation that the British security forces . . . 'tortured' suspected Irish Republican Army (IRA) internees" (Hurwitz, 1995, p. 301).

> These methods were termed "sensory-deprivation" . . . and they were designed to elicit information from the internees . . . one of the major issues was not whether these occurred, but rather, whether such behavior and additional actions by the British government constituted a violation of the European Convention. (Hurwitz, 1995, p. 301)

Great Britain eventually "admitted fault, stopped the practice of sensory deprivation," and made financial compensation to the victims.

In February 1972, in Londonderry (Northern Ireland), following a civil rights demonstration, British soldiers shot to death 13 people and wounded 16 unarmed civilians. This incident, generally referred to as Bloody Sunday, was the subject of a highly publicized inquiry that culminated in the Widgery Report, which, in turn, was perceived as a whitewash of British army activities during this incident. In 1997, new material emerged in connection with Bloody Sunday that further implicated the British army in a planned act of murder (Ross, 2000a).

Human Rights Violations in Canada

Canada, which has an international reputation of being a peace-loving country, or peaceable kingdom (Ross, 1995d), is rarely accused of human rights violations. Over the past two decades the country has been under scrutiny by the worldwide community with respect to police use of excessive force and "degrading treatment or punishment of its indigenous peoples" (e.g., U.S. Department of State, 2002).

SAFEGUARDING HUMAN RIGHTS

In general, there are five areas where the protection of human rights has been expressed or implemented: philosophy, treaties, state-level documents and bodies, regional bodies, and international agencies and documents.

Philosophical Background

Human rights doctrines can be traced back to the Code of Hammurabi, through religious laws, and then to the Magna Carta. The concept of human rights originated during the period of Enlightenment in Western society, especially through the scholarship of English philosophers such as Hobbes and Locke. Well-known American statesmen, such as Thomas Jefferson and Thomas Paine, contributed to the formulation of human rights law. It has been expressed in various legal documents, including the English Bill of Rights, the American Declaration of Independence, the U.S. Constitution and Bill of Rights, and the French Declaration of the Rights of Man and of the Citizen.

Treaties

The history of attempts at safeguarding against human rights abuses began around the time of the treaty of Westphalia (1648) when John Locke and Hugo Grotius, among others, began promoting the Natural Law principles of inalienable human rights to life, liberty, and property. Although these basic principles were firmly in place in many countries, blatant violations existed in the form of slavery and genocide (Bennett, 1991, p. 372). As a result, in 1815, the United Kingdom urged states to develop treaties suppressing the slave trade. During the following century, agreements were enacted protecting individuals from various injustices. A significant advance culminated in the peace treaties of 1919, which guaranteed fair treatment for inhabitants of mandated territories and for particular racial minorities in Eastern and Central Europe. At the end of World War I, the League of Nations established the International Labor Organization (ILO), which was responsible for improving working conditions throughout the world's ongoing industrialization and for promoting workers' rights (Akehurst, 1987, p. 76).

Why would a country want to monitor human rights violations in other states? A number of reasons can be suggested. Perhaps it genuinely cares about the welfare of others. Alternatively, the monitoring state may worry about the economic climate for doing business in that country. It might worry about a refugee or immigrant problem at home that is caused by the exodus of individuals from the state where the abuse is taking place. The monitoring state may also see it as a form of public relations in the world arena, a way to gain favorable exposure. Moreover, the monitoring may serve as a rationale for invasion. And finally, it may be a means of nonviolent payback in the court of world opinion.

Country-Level Departments

Attempts at safeguarding human rights have occurred at primarily four levels: national, regional, international, and nongovernmental. At the national level, states monitor civil rights abuses through such governmental bodies as federal, provincial, or state civil rights commissions. Many countries' constitutions contain statements on human rights and have commissions to investigate alleged abuses, although states often cannot and do not monitor human rights abuses that they themselves have generated (e.g., Hurwitz, 1995, p. 284). Some countries will delegate the monitoring of human rights abuses to their State Department or Ministry of External or Foreign Affairs. The U.S. State Department, for example, regularly brings to the world's attention human rights violators. And during treaty negotiations, trade and official missions, and official visits to other countries, human rights violations may become an issue. This was the case in September 1995, during the visit of former First Lady Hillary Rodham Clinton to the People's Republic of China.

Regional Efforts

Regional organizations also contribute to the protection of human rights, most notably the Council of Europe, which has existed since 1950 (Bennett, 1991, p. 374; Hurwitz, 1995). In the United Nations, diverse ideologies and interests, and a general lack of trust, make human rights agreements difficult to reach. Regional levels of agreement have proven easier to obtain where greater amounts of trust exist among participating states and where common values and interests are shared regionally (Akehurst, 1987, pp. 78-79).

The Council of Europe, for example, investigates complaints and works toward conciliatory solutions to a dispute. If that proves unsuccessful, the case is referred to the Committee of Ministers, which may rule that the violating state must rectify the abuses. In extreme cases, expulsion from the organization may occur (Akehurst, 1987, p. 80).

In Europe, the Helsinki Accords of 1975, which was the culmination of the Conference on Security and Cooperation in Europe, provided another gain in regional efforts at controlling human rights abuses. Although not a treaty, and lacking adequate mechanisms for enforcement, it includes respect for human rights and fundamental freedoms, "including freedom of thought, conscience, religion, or belief" (Bennett, 1991, p. 375).

The atrocities of mass murder and concentration camps as official state policy during World War II provided the impetus for the universalization and internationalization of human rights (Bennett, 1991, p. 372). The United Nations Charter, declaring the promotion of human rights, was "the watershed document that marked the beginning of . . . expansion of human rights as an appropriate area for international concern" (Bennett, 1991, p. 372).

International Bodies

Undoubtedly the founding of the United Nations and its "Charter pledges on human rights were circumscribed; the duty was to promote human rights, not to guarantee them as a matter of law for all citizens" (Robertson, 2000, p. 26). The most important (and controversial) document has been the UN Declaration on Human Rights. Although each of these statements varies, collectively they support the ideal of inalienable rights and freedoms that supersede policies and practices of specific states and governments (Hagan, 1990, p. 423). Article 55 of the UN Charter mandates that the United Nations shall promote "universal respect for, and observance of, human rights and fundamental freedoms for all without distinction as to race, sex, language or religion" (Akehurst, 1987, p. 76). Buttressing the language of this article, United Nations members pledged to act independently and cooperatively for the promotion of human rights. Even though gains have been made, the Charter's language undoubtedly leaves some discretion to states about fulfilling their obligations, and in some countries few human rights advances have occurred (Akehurst, 1987, p. 76). Regardless, the General Assembly and Trusteeship Council are obligated to promote human rights, and, through the Economic and Social Council, the rights of women and minorities in particular have been addressed, although, as with most attempts at promoting human rights, with mixed results (Bennett, 1991, p. 373).

The Universal Declaration of Human Rights, a resolution passed by the UN General Assembly on December 10, 1948, provides first for civil and political rights and second for economic, social, and cultural rights, including "the right to social security, to full employment and fair conditions of work, to an adequate standard of living, to education and to participation in the cultural life of the community" (Akehurst, 1987, pp. 77-78).

Although General Assembly resolutions are legally nonbinding, the Declaration of Human Rights has had a major impact on human rights standards worldwide. Today it is widely known and serves to advance a "common standard or conduct for the protection and expansion of individual rights" (Bennett, 1991, p. 373). Furthermore, the Declaration has been cited in various court opinions,

> has been partially incorporated into at least forty-five national constitutional documents (including the [former] Soviet and Chinese), has influenced

national legislation, has been referred to in international treaties, and is constantly alluded to in the United Nations debates and documents. It may be reasonably argued that the Universal Declaration, through this usage and as an explication of Charter purposes and obligations, has progressively attained the status of international law. (Bennett, 1991, p. 373)

Immediately after its adoption, a movement was initiated to rewrite the Declaration into treaties or conventions that would bind states subscribing to the United Nations Declaration of Human Rights. Even though many differences emerged across the years of effort, finally, on December 16, 1966, after 12 years of discussion, the United Nations completed the drafting of two treaties designed to transform the principles of the Universal Declaration of Human Rights into binding and detailed rules of law: the International Covenant on Civil and Political Rights, and the International Covenant on Economic, Social and Cultural Rights (Akehurst, 1987, p. 81; Bennett, 1991).

The documents became effective in 1976 (Akehurst, 1987). Since that time, the covenants on human rights have been extended to more specialized treaties on various aspects of rights, including protecting women's rights and refugees' status, and denouncing slavery, forced labor, torture, South Africa's apartheid, and discrimination in employment and education (Bennett, 1991, p. 374).

Despite the establishing and signing of numerous treaties, conventions, and declarations on human rights, not one individual was convicted of abuses until 1977. This is not because there were not numerous examples of human rights violations taking place during this time period. Essentially, "The Human Rights Commission remained tight-lipped about breaches of the Universal Declaration, or the Genocide and Geneva Conventions, by any government that was a member of the UN" (Robertson, 2000, pp. 39-40), especially about abuses committed by the CIA or Stalinist Soviet Union. One of the setbacks has traditionally been that some leaders in many countries invoke the problem of insensitivity to local customs, Western imperialism, and cultural relativism. In 1975, as a result of Pinochet's regime, the United Nations signed the Declaration Against Torture (Robertson, 2000, chap. 2).

Beyond these public national, regional, and international agencies, private groups also have been active in promoting and safeguarding human rights. Indeed, the United Nations Commission on Human Rights sessions typically include the participation of several international nongovernmental organizations (INGOs) in the proceedings (Bennett, 1991, p. 375). Representatives of these private organizations not only attend the meetings but frequently "invoke their privilege of addressing the sessions on such subjects as apartheid in South Africa, violations of human rights in Israeli-occupied territories, the use of torture in several countries, or the problem of missing persons in Latin American states" (Bennett, 1991, p. 376). Among these private participants, the most respected and also among the most vilified by the regimes accused of gross human rights violations are Amnesty International and Human Rights Watch.

Although it is difficult to identify human rights violations in advanced industrialized democracies (Ross, 2000c), several well-publicized examples have taken place. During the Cold War, in the United States in particular, there were several "mind control" experiments sponsored by prominent state criminogenic agencies on unsuspecting individuals, both citizens and employees of the agency.

> Using code names such as Bluebird, Artichoke, and MKULTRA, the CIA, FBI, and military in the 1950s experimented with various behavioral control devices and interrogation techniques including . . . drugs, polygraphs, hypnosis, shock therapy, surgery, and radiation. This involved secret experiments on unknowing citizens and, when harm took place, a cover-up. (Hagan, 1997, p. 36)

These tests were not restricted to the United States:

> A Canadian teenager seeking medical treatment for an arthritic leg was subjected to LSD, electroshock therapy, and forced to listen to hours of taped messages . . . as part of a series of bizarre experiments financed by the CIA and conducted by a former president of the American Psychiatric Association. Over 100 Canadians from 1957 to 1961 were unknowing guinea pigs, causing them much psychiatric harm. (Hagan, 1997, p. 36)

Starting in the mid-1940s, various federal departments involved in nuclear research "conducted experiments on U.S. citizens, including injecting them with plutonium, radium, and uranium" (Hagan, 1997, p. 360). These findings, revealed in a 1986 House Energy and Commerce Subcommittee hearing, documented that this practice continued for a 30-year period (Kauzlarich & Kramer, 1998).

NONGOVERNMENTAL ORGANIZATIONS
THAT PROTECT HUMAN RIGHTS

There are a number of nongovernmental organizations that exist to monitor and campaign on behalf of human rights. During the past two decades grass-roots progressive organizations, activists, and progressive-minded lawyers have taken up the cause of human rights. Two prominent nongovernmental organizations (in danger of becoming over-bureaucratized and distant from their membership and constituency) have been working in this area: Amnesty International (AI) and Human Rights Watch (HRW).

HRW is dedicated "to protecting the human rights of people around the world." It works "with victims and activists to prevent discrimination, to uphold political freedom, to protect people from inhumane conduct in wartime, and to bring offenders to justice." HRW "investigate[s] and expose[s] human rights violations and hold[s] abusers accountable." It "challenge[s] governments and those who hold power to end abusive practices and respect international human rights law" ("About," 2002).

Originally founded in 1978 as Helsinki Watch, Human Rights Watch/Helsinki, in response to a call for support from embattled local groups in Moscow, Warsaw, and Prague,

> had been set up to monitor compliance with the human rights provisions of the landmark Helsinki accords. A few years later, when the Reagan administration argued that human rights abuses by right-wing "authoritarian" governments were more tolerable than those of left-wing "totalitarian" governments, HRW formed Americas Watch . . . to counter this double standard.

By 1987, the organization had "honed a powerful set of techniques—painstaking documentation of abuses and hard-hitting advocacy in the press and with governments—and put them to use all over the world as Human Rights Watch." Currently, HRW is "the largest U.S.-based human rights organization" ("Information," 2002).

"Through its reports and advocacy efforts, Human Rights Watch works to stop abuses." In order to accomplish its mission, HRW's "staff of over 100 regional experts, lawyers and linguists helps explain why abuses break out and—most important—what must be done to stop them." HRW seeks to damage abusers' "reputation and legitimacy if they violate the rights of their people."

HRW "seek[s] to curb abuses regardless of whether the victims are well-known political activists or those of lesser visibility such as factory workers, peasants, farmers, undocumented migrants, women forced into prostitution, street children, or domestic workers." The organization "also address[es] such war-related abuses as indiscriminate shelling or the use of rape or starvation as weapons of war—no matter which side in a conflict is responsible."

HRW "also presses for withdrawal of military, economic and diplomatic support from governments that are regularly abusive." It

> conduct[s] frequent investigations in countries where abuses take place. In a number of hot spots, [it] maintains offices to gather information on an ongoing basis . . . interview victims and witnesses of human rights abuse . . . meet with government officials, opposition leaders, local human rights groups, church officials, labor leaders, journalists, lawyers, relief groups, doctors, and others with reliable first-hand information on the current human rights situation. If a country refuses to allow us to enter, . . . we find other ways of obtaining information to compile as complete and accurate a picture as we can. ("Information," 2002)

Amnesty International "is a worldwide campaigning movement that works to promote all the human rights enshrined in the Universal Declaration of Human Rights and other international standards." Originally established in 1960 in London, England, it slowly expanded until AI membership became worldwide. Its initial focus was on "prisoners of conscience," those incarcerated for their political beliefs. Later, AI would send observers to countries with political detainees and attend trials of those charged with political offenses. In particular, Amnesty International "campaigns to free all prisoners of conscience; ensure fair and prompt trials for political prisoners; abolish the death penalty, torture and other cruel treatment of prisoners; end political killings and 'disappearances'; and oppose human rights abuses by opposition groups" (Amnesty International, 2002).

AI "has around a million members and supporters in 162 countries and territories. Activities range from public demonstrations to letter-writing, from human rights education to fund-raising concerts, from individual appeals on a particular case to global campaigns on a particular issue." Needless to say, the backbone of the lobbying efforts is its letter-writing campaigns to highly placed officials in the countries where detainees are being held. AI also issues annual reports on the state of human rights throughout the world.

This organization "is impartial and independent of any government, political persuasion or religious creed. Amnesty International is financed largely by subscriptions and donations from its worldwide membership." The organization has earned the respect of many international bodies, it now has what is called consultative status at many world bodies (e.g., the UN, UNESCO, etc.), and it won the Nobel Peace Prize (Amnesty International, 2002).

Finally, almost every advanced industrialized democracy has a major civil liberties organization. For the protection of civil liberties and rights in America, it is the American Civil Liberties Union, the Canadian Civil Liberties Association for their neighbor to the north, and the National Association of Civil Liberties in the United Kingdom.

WAR CRIMES

"International law has sought to regulate wars in two ways: initially, by restricting the justifications for waging them, and (when that failed) by prescribing rules for conducting them humanely" (Robertson, 2000, p. 167). Unfortunately, these laws are replete with inherent contradictions and are selective because some parties benefit from them. The rules of war don't do well in "low intensity civil war or internecine struggle in which one state seeks to suppress rebel militias or armed dissidents" (Robertson, 2000, p. 168).

After World War II, both high-ranking Nazi (German) and Japanese commanders were subjected to war crimes trials in Nuremberg, Germany, and Tokyo, Japan, respectively. Recently, the UN International Criminal Tribunal for the former Yugoslavia has been investigating war crimes in connection with the Srebrenica massacre, Kosovo. Although the issue of war crimes affects most advanced industrialized countries because they take responsibility for conducting the affairs, and for marshaling the resources in order for the tribunals to take place, rarely have these countries been charged with these kinds of offenses.

CHANGES IN HUMAN RIGHTS PRACTICE

During the 1970s, disappearances, torture, and death squads operated in several South American countries. Unfortunately, many of the perpetrators (i.e., torturers, killers, and their supervisors) were granted amnesties or pardons. A similar fate can be observed in the so-called Truth Commissions, which have taken place in only a handful of countries (Robertson, 2000, chap. 8).

As a result of the genocides in Yugoslavia, The Hague Tribunal was established to prosecute those charged with war crimes: "many argued it would demonstrate how war crimes were committed only by a handful of evil individuals, thus relieving their countrymen from the stigma of 'collective responsibility' for crimes against humanity" (Robertson, 2000, p. 417). In the context of Yugoslavia, and the genocide of Croatians, the UN Security Council was and is practically ineffectual in matters of international human rights. NATO had considerable difficulties in being able to force the surrender of Milosevic and highly placed Serbian generals. Courts are severely circumscribed in what they can do in the matter of human rights violations. "There is no court as yet to stop a state which murders and extirpates its own people; for them, if the Security Council fails to reach superpower agreement, the only salvation can come through other states exercising the right of humanitarian intervention" (Robertson, 2000, p. 420).

Another recent example of human rights violations was the case of East Timor, which "was important because an invasion force was mustered which was prepared not only to kill but to be killed in the cause of human rights" (Robertson, 2000, p. 425), but this force would not be allowed entrance until after countless East Timorese were slaughtered by the Indonesian army and the militias it backed. The problem of East Timor demonstrates the futility of the International Court of Justice (ICJ). In 1975 the case came before the ICJ, which reviewed the atrocities that had occurred as a result of the Indonesian referendum on independence. The United Nations failed in its oversight of East Timor, but acted properly both before and after the atrocities were under way (Robertson, 2000).

In 2001, the arrest of Pinochet by British authorities spelled an end to the age-old privilege of impunity. No longer would diplomatic status prevent one from being detained, arrested, and even tried.

SUMMARY

Safeguarding and promoting human rights is a paradox of sorts. On the one hand, lessons from history inform us that the need to protect human rights is apparent. On the other hand, the state—the entity with the power, force, and law to protect human rights—is usually the perpetrator or a silent partner in infringements on those rights. Furthermore, countries are protective of their own sovereignty, which complicates matters because guaranteeing protection of human rights has traditionally fallen solely to domestic jurisdictions.

International efforts are likely perceived as external or even revolutionary and typically are resisted by managers and agents of sovereign states. "The international community and regional organizations are ill-equipped to enforce uniform standards of human rights on individual countries. Their methods fall short of compulsion and involve primarily persuasion, publicity, and the pressure of public opinion" (Bennett, 1991, p. 379). States accused of violating human rights often respond by ignoring the charges or by blaming their accusers of human rights atrocities in their own countries. As long as differences persist in basic values, definitions, and value systems, the adoption of universally accepted standards of human rights will remain difficult to achieve and implement.

TEST QUESTIONS

Multiple-Choice

1. If you were a suspected member of the Irish Republican Army and felt that your human rights were violated, in which human rights court would you expect to get the greatest amount of justice?
   a. municipal
   b. provincial
   c. national
   d. regional
   e. international

2. What is Amnesty International?
   a. a drug rehabilitation network
   b. an NGO that monitors human rights abuses
   c. an agency that helps Vietnam War draft dodgers
   d. an organization that campaigns for the elimination of prisons in the United States
   e. Phil Collins's backup band

3. Where were the Nuremberg Trials held?
   a. Israel
   b. United States
   c. United Kingdom
   d. Austria
   e. Germany

4. Human rights doctrines can be traced back to
   a. Code of Hammurabi
   b. Magna Carta
   c. Code of Human Rights
   d. a and b only
   e. none of the above

5. The notion of human rights has been expressed in which legal documents?
   a. English Bill of Rights
   b. U.S. Constitution
   c. American Declaration of Independence
   d. French Declaration of the Rights of Man and of the Citizen
   e. all of the above

6. When did attempts regarding safeguarding human rights among countries begin?
   a. World War I
   b. Cold War
   c. Treaty of Westphalia
   d. all of the above
   e. none of the above

7. In the United States we can probably trace human rights violations back to
   a. the War of 1812
   b. internment of European-born civilians during World War I
   c. forced removal of Japanese Americans during World War II
   d. execution of Julius and Ethel Rosenberg
   e. none of the above

Short Answer

1. List four political philosophers or theorists who contributed to the development of human rights thought.

2. Which body passed the Universal Declaration of Human Rights?

3. List three reasons why a country would want to monitor the human rights violations of another state.

4. What was Bloody Sunday?

❧ TEN ❧

STATE VIOLENCE

S tate violence[1] as a form of political crime generally consists of illegal, physically harmful actions committed by a country's coercive organizations (i.e., police, national security agencies, and military) against individuals and groups.[2] Regardless of the political system, victims of state violence generally are actual or suspected criminals; political opponents (dissidents) of the government or regime in power (e.g., activists, trade unionists, and peasants); or people of color, ethnic or religious groups, and immigrants. Such violence can be both domestic and foreign in nature (e.g., against another country, especially during war).[3] Here, however, our discussion is limited to what takes place in Canada, United States, and the United Kingdom.

Nine principal interrelated actions are subsumed under state violence: disappearances or kidnappings, death squad activity, torture, deaths in custody, police violence or excessive force, police riots, police use of deadly force, terrorism, and genocide. Even though state violence has occurred in all types of political systems, by all kinds of state coercive organizations, the relative frequency of each subtype varies across political systems. For example—and directly germane to this discussion—disappearances/kidnappings, death squad activity, genocide, and state terrorism rarely occur within advanced industrialized democracies. They are more likely to be present in lesser-developed countries with authoritarian or totalitarian leadership (Berman & Clark, 1982). In short, rich countries repress or imprison their dissidents, but poor countries murder because they cannot afford internment.

When state violence becomes public, it often is interpreted and sometimes appropriately labeled as a human rights violation (see Chapter 9). Thus, much of the literature, theory, and controls that are applicable to human rights are pertinent to the problem of state violence.

Our knowledge of state violence is limited. Much information about this type of crime is not public; thus few people ever learn about these actions. Data tend to be unreliable and are collected in an unsystematic fashion. This minimizes our ability to take appropriate actions to prevent, minimize, or stop this behavior. In fact, it appears as if the media's focus is on oppositional rather than state violence as a form of political crime.

Most information about this political illegality comes from eyewitnesses or victims of state violence. Their stories may be or appear exaggerated and biased because of the physical or psychological trauma they have experienced or due to their own political agendas. The appearance of bias may also result from media sensationalism.

Incidents of state violence have been exposed and documented in popular and alternative media accounts, governmental commission reports, coroner's inquests, autopsy reports, academic treatments, and the reports of nongovernmental bodies (e.g., international monitoring agencies like Amnesty International and Human Rights Watch).

Four principal organizations produce relevant data on state violence: Amnesty International, Freedom House, Human Rights Watch, and the U.S. Department of State. Although all of these sources report some of these activities, each suffers from a number of problems, including access to data, a lack of comprehensiveness due to unsystematic use of time periods, data that are difficult to disaggregate by year, the trouble associated with systematically comparing countries, and decisions that often are guided by organizational imperatives and ideological constraints that depart from the strict dissemination of information on state violence (Mitchell, Stohl, Carleton, & Lopez, 1986). In order to comprehend this type of political crime better, the definitions, history, and some causes focusing on torture, deaths in custody, police riots, police use of deadly force, and genocide are reviewed.

TORTURE

Torture includes

> any act by which severe pain or suffering whether physical or mental is intentionally inflicted by or at the instigation of a public official on a person for

such purposes as obtaining from him or a third person information or confession, punishing him for an act he had committed or is suspected of having committed, or intimidating him or other persons. (Millet, 1994, p. 13)

Torture involves such physical techniques as beatings, burnings, dry sub-marining,[4] and electroshock. Authorities can use torture as both a specific and a general deterrent. Furthermore, it is used as "punishment for undetermined guilt," to "extract money from the victim or because somebody has given the police money to thrash him/her," and as revenge (Balagopal, 1986, p. 2029). It assumes "particularly vicious forms when the suspect has done injury to the police themselves" (Balagopal, 1986, p. 2029). The scholarly literature on torture has ascertained three dominant causes (albeit at the individual level): psychoanalytic processes (Daraki-Mallet, 1976), obedience to authority (Miligram, 1974, 1977), and finally, obedience to the authority of violence (Haritos-Fatouros, 1988).

The literature on torture is problematic because it is difficult to distin-guish which government agencies are responsible for this gruesome act and to generalize from one situation of torture to another; dominant causal expla-nations have focused on individuals and avoided structural issues. There is a paucity of reliable data because many reports of torture are based on victim and witness accounts of questionable reliability. The most prominent examples of torture that have come to attention during the contemporary period and in advanced industrialized countries have been the British military's treatment of real or alleged members of the Irish Republican Army (Hurwitz, 1995; Ross, 2000a).

DEATHS IN CUSTODY

Persons who die in custody, whether in a police lock-up or a prison, may have been previously involved in interpersonal violence with other citizens prior to arrest, with law enforcement/prison personnel, or with other prisoners. Investigations of deaths in custody are complicated by the state officials' common but questionable explanation that the victim(s) died because of "mis-adventure" or had committed suicide, which disregards the state's obligation to secure the safety and security of an individual's life while in custody (e.g., Hazelhurst, 1991; Home Affairs Committee, 1980; Scraton & Chadwick, 1985). Balagopal (1986) suggests the mono-causal explanation that police torture is used arbitrarily and results in fatalities, not because a rational use of torture leads to serious and even fatal excesses, but because the normal methods and intensity of torture naturally and necessarily lead to death in a given combination of circumstances: "the lock-up is exceptionally insanitary [sic], the victim is of weak bodily health, does not get adequate food while in lock-up, is dispirited and demoralized by a false or morally unjust accusation, is deprived of proper medical attention, etc." (p. 2028).

Reports of deaths in custody are based on autopsy evidence and commissions of inquiry whose reliability is often debatable. The medical examiners are typically forced to gather their evidence in a highly politicized environment, usually with the threat of a lawsuit motivating the respective parties. Moreover, explanations rely on many of the same factors as torture and do not explore a variety of other possible causes. In the contemporary period, there has been an overabundance of deaths in custody of aboriginal peoples in Australia and of native peoples in the United States and Canada (Correctional Services of Canada, 1992; Hazelhurst, 1991). Quite often the official ruling is "Death by Misadventure," which places the responsibility on the individual or victim who engaged in risky behavior.

POLICE RIOTS

Although occurring relatively infrequently, police riots involve the rampaging of police, primarily riot squads, during public strike and protest conditions. They take place in both large and small cities (Hahn & Feagin, 1970; Marx, 1970a, 1970b; Reiner, 1980; Stark, 1972). Victims of such state police riots have traditionally been students and striking workers.

Despite the volume of reports and studies, researchers of police riots have not specified causes for their commission beyond that of lower-ranking police following the orders of superiors, poor training, and the stress experienced by officers in tense situations (ironically, mass behavior and collective action explanations have not been used).

During the 1960s and 1970s in the United States, for example, there were several police riots that were responses to student demonstrations against the Vietnam War and to civil rights protests, or to reactions to police brutality. These were largely centered in the big cities, like New York, Chicago, and Los Angeles (Richards & Avey, 2000; Ross, 2000b).

In Canada (Ross, 1995b) police riots are rare events. The majority of events have surrounded large-scale protests in which the police were deployed and then overreacted. Many of these have been the subject of government inquiries.

In the United Kingdom, for example, during the 1980s police riots took place against Caribbeans, Asians, and striking miners (Scraton, 1985). Since the early 1960s, the United Kingdom has experienced many police-citizen confrontations, some of which resulted in considerable worldwide attention. In cases where police violence in Britain has been the focus of study, it is usually addressed in the context of riots, strikes, and deaths in custody. For example, the literature covers the police role in the 1980s race riots (e.g., Benyon, 1984; Cowell & Young, 1982; Fowler, 1979; Kettle & Hodges, 1982); the 1984 miners' strike (e.g., Coulter, Miller, & Walker, 1984; Fine & Millar, 1985); other labor disputes (e.g., Geary, 1985); and deaths in custody (e.g., Scraton & Chadwick, 1985).

Research aimed at determining explanations for police violence as a form of political crime is hampered by limited data. Furthermore, most research is descriptive and seems not to have progressed beyond case study analyses. Anecdotal evidence suggests that at least in the United States, police riots have not been as frequent as they were during the 1960s ghetto riots.

POLICE USE OF DEADLY FORCE

Admittedly, the majority of people in advanced industrialized countries who are killed by the police die as a result of law enforcement use of deadly force. These incidents have been given attention in popular and alternative media reports and governmental inquiries largely due to the relative ease of documenting such acts of police violence. A plethora of variables has been examined as plausible causes of police use of deadly force. The most significant finding is that administrative posture and policy on the use of deadly force are the most important determinants of the number of citizens shot and killed by police (Fyfe, 1979; Sherman, 1980a, 1980b).

Nevertheless, research literature on the causes of police use of deadly force points out various criticisms, primarily issues of internal validity and disagreements over the accuracy of the measurements of dependent variables (i.e., justifiable homicides vs. shots fired; Binder & Fridell, 1984;

Binder & Scharf, 1980; Blumberg, 1982; Fridell, 1985; Fyfe, 1978; Geller, 1982; Scharf & Binder, 1983). Based on a review of 20 articles, Horvath (1987) concludes that most research has been carried out only in "large cities and large urban areas"; "has involved only incidents in which fatalities of citizens occurred"; and that "there are substantial methodological differences between studies making it difficult to draw meaningful comparisons or to generalize from any one group of apparently similar findings" (p. 226). Moreover, there are other police techniques that can cause death but are rarely included in deadly force statistics (e.g., choke holds, death by baton). Finally, most studies have been limited to the United States.[5]

GENOCIDE

Genocide is the systematic killing of an ethnic, racial, religious, or cultural group (Kuper, 1985). Historically, one of the most salient genocides was that of the Holocaust:

> At its peak, Nazi Germany and its allies occupied virtually all of Europe, except for Britain and part of Russia. Under its fanatical policies of racial purity, Germany rounded up and exterminated six million Jews and millions of others, including homosexuals, Gypsies, Communists, and others. These mass murders, now known as the Holocaust, along with the sheer scale of war unleashed by Nazi aggression, are considered among the greatest crimes against humanity in history. Responsible German officers faced justice in the Nuremberg Tribunal after the war. (Goldstein, 1996, p. 39)

This famous trial "established that participants can be held accountable for war crimes they commit. German officers defended their actions as 'just following orders' but this was rejected; the officers were punished, some executed for their war crimes" (Goldstein, 1996, p. 299). The trials led to the genocide and torture conventions and the placement of human rights issues within international jurisdiction. Nevertheless, "the pledges of world leaders after that experience to 'never again' allow genocide . . . have been found wanting as genocide recurred in the post-Cold War era in Bosnia and Rwanda" (Goldstein, 1996, p. 39). Similar genocides have occurred throughout human history, including the recent troubles in Rwanda, Indonesia, and Kosovo. However, in the context of advanced industrialized countries and during the period of investigation, genocides, in the strictest use of the term, have not occurred.[6]

SUMMARY

Of the different types of state violence reviewed above, deaths in custody and police use of deadly force are the most prominent in the advanced industrialized countries. In short, police violence depends on many of the factors articulated in more general studies of police behavior, misconduct, deviance, organizational tolerance, and complaints against the police. These causes can be classified into individual, situational, organizational, community, and legal attributes. Many of these factors interact with each other to create complicated explanations for police violence.

The bulk of work on police violence deals with its causes (e.g., Reiss, 1968; Worden, 1995). This research can also be divided into two categories: studies examining a broad range of police violence, and work focusing on particular forms. Although some scholars (e.g., Feld, 1971; Manning, 1980; Westley, 1953, 1970) examined the causes of police violence in general, most focused on single factors. Concurrently, causes for police violence are often broken down into internal and external factors (e.g., Stark, 1972). The former entails influences such as a patrol officer's personality, attitudes and values, working environment, police culture, relationship to the courts, and professionalization (e.g., Kania & Mackay, 1977).

The latter usually includes community structure and social polarization (e.g., Feld, 1971). General studies have not demarcated the contribution of different influences in causing police violence. Often ignored is the fact that police violence is indirectly connected to frequency of street stops, crime in a community, number of police deployed in a particular area, and number and type of arrests. In short, the greater the number of these indirect factors, the more opportunities available to the police to engage in violence.

Several individual, situational, organizational, community, and legal attributes have been posited and/or tested as causes leading a police officer to use violence. All said, there are several problems with the general literature dealing with the causes of police violence. Because the literature primarily has a U.S. focus, it remains unknown whether its conclusions can be generalized. The data are limited in scope, usually collected in the context of observational studies, and/or often not comparable among jurisdictions. Furthermore, the work does not examine attempts to remove the presumed causes of such political crimes.

Nevertheless, building on the previous theoretical discussions, there are organizational norms that reinforce the use of violence against certain types of individuals. People who come from certain social classes or religious, ethnic, or racial groups are often selected, and rationalizations are developed to support abuse against them. Recently this type of behavior was made visible in the trial of American sports figure O. J. Simpson and the testimony and scandal surrounding Mark Fuhrman, the Los Angeles Police Department detective who testified in the case (Barak, 1996).

In addition, there are strong structural arguments that support the idea that state coercive organizations exist to maintain the dominant political order (Ross, 1998a). In short, a municipal police force was established due to the influence of the wealthy class of London who wanted their lives and property to be protected against rogues. Moreover, the majority of police officers come from working- or middle-class backgrounds. In the United States historically, the police have repressed African Americans and Hispanics and have suppressed labor unrest and working-class interests, all the while supporting ongoing capitalist industrialization and growth (e.g., Center for Research on Criminal Justice, 1977; Harring, 1983; Ross, 1998b).

NOTES

1. This chapter builds on Ross (2001).

2. In the main, there are three perpetrators of state violence: individuals possessing the force of law through their occupations as state agents and who abuse their lawful positions; organizations within the state, such as the police, military, and national security units; and states advancing an official, yet more than likely unspoken, policy of violence and repression. The relative contribution of each of these state apparatuses varies depending on the country and its political system.

3. This discussion avoids the thorny issue of the illegal use of war that is waged in violation of the United Nations Charter, which states when and under what conditions a country may engage in war.

4. Placing an individual's head under water for a short period of time, for example, in a bucket of water or in a toilet bowl.

5. Exceptions to this are Bernheim (1990) and Chevigny (1990). For a legal history of the right of police to use deadly force, see Sherman (1980b); see Brown (1984) for research on other police uses of deadly force.

6. Although some writers have suggested that the policies and practices directed against African Americans (Johnson & Leighton, 1999) and Native Americans (Churchill, 1997) are tantamount to genocide, this argument may stretch the empirical/ scholarly boundaries of what is meant by the term.

TEST QUESTIONS

Multiple-Choice

1. The majority of people who are killed in advanced industrialized countries by the police die as a result of
   a. torture
   b. genocide
   c. police riots
   d. police use of deadly force
   e. what takes place in custody

2. Victims in police riots have traditionally been
   a. students
   b. striking workers
   c. business owners
   d. both a and b
   e. none of the above

3. Deaths in custody are primarily the result of
   a. beatings by police
   b. beatings by other inmates
   c. assaults by correctional officers
   d. hangings
   e. overdoses

4. What is the systematic killing of a cultural, ethnic, racial, or religious group?
   a. terrorism
   b. genocide
   c. torture
   d. death squad activity
   e. disappearances

5. Which organization does not produce data on state violence?
   a. Amnesty International
   b. Center for Public Integrity
   c. Freedom House
   d. Human Rights Watch
   e. All of them do

6. Data collected on state violence are
   a. systematic
   b. detailed
   c. unsystematic
   d. depends on the source
   e. none of the above

7. Most studies of police use of deadly force have been limited to
   a. Great Britain
   b. Canada
   c. United States
   d. Australia
   e. New Zealand

Short Answer

1. What are three criticisms of existing research conducted on police use of deadly force?

2. Nine principal interrelated actions are subsumed by state violence. Name four of them.

3. What are the three dominant causes (put forward by scholars) for torture?

4. What are two ways that international law has sought to regulate wars?

ELEVEN

STATE-CORPORATE CRIME

State-corporate crime, a recent concept in the ongoing understanding of white-collar, corporate, and governmental crime, results from inter-actions among corporate and state policies, practices, and outcomes. Such crimes take place when these organizations (in both the private and the public sectors) pursue goals that result in crime including—but not limited to—injury, disease, death, and eco-system destruction. Most people have little idea how and why corporations get established. Before continuing it might be instructive to understand why individuals, businesses, and corporations form corporations. In general, corporations are a vehicle or structure created to raise large sums of money, have more favorable tax laws (i.e., pay less taxes), and limit organizational liability in case the corporation is ever sued.

State-corporate crimes are committed by individuals who abuse their state authority or who fail to exercise it when working with people and organizations in the private sector. Their actions and inactions, and the resulting social harms, emanate from these mutually reinforcing interactions among corporate and state policies, practices, and outcomes.

DEFINITIONAL AND CONCEPTUAL ISSUES

State-corporate crime first was defined as

> a form of organizational misconduct that occurs at the interstices of corpora-tions and governments. Within a capitalist economy, such crimes involve the

active participation of two or more organizations, at least one of which is in the civil sector and the other in the state sector. Thus, state-corporate crimes are the harmful consequences of a deviant inter-organizational relationship between business and government. (Kramer, 1992, p. 215)

State-corporate crimes are illegal or socially injurious actions that result from a mutually reinforcing interaction between (1) policies and/or practices in pursuit of the goals of one or more institutions of political governance and (2) policies and/or practices in pursuit of the goals of one or more institutions of economic production and distribution. (Aulette & Michalowski, 1993, p. 175)[1]

Although first applied to the Space Shuttle *Challenger* case, the concept has much wider application and is used here to explain further state actions that are criminal domestically, internationally, and—following Sutherland's lead (1949b)—socially injurious, but not defined by the state as criminal. The state's complicitous role in state-corporate transgressions is especially pertinent regarding acts of commission and omission against less powerful forces and those groups that traditionally have been victimized by state crimes, namely workers and political dissidents (e.g., Friedrichs, 1995).

In addition, this conceptualization of state-corporate crime is organizational, recognizing, however, that individual actors and their interactions within the strictures of organizations and organizations' powerful cultures of competition within which individuals function have a strong bearing on the propensity for corporations and states to act in a criminal fashion (Kramer, 1982, 1992).

Although the term *state-corporate crime* has only recently been applied to specific cases where corporate and state policies have interacted to produce criminal consequences, history is replete with examples of this kind of behavior. These examples simply had not previously been analyzed or labeled as state-corporate crimes.

TYPOLOGY

Because the field of state-corporate crime is relatively new, the opportunity to classify different kinds of state-corporate crimes is in its infancy. To date, the only distinction that exists is between state-initiated corporate crime and state-facilitated corporate crime (Kramer & Michalowski, 1990). In the former, businesses commit "organizational deviance at the direction of, or with the tacit approval of, the government" (p. 191). In the latter, "government regulatory institutions fail to restrain deviant business activities, because of direct collusion between business and government, or because they adhere to shared goals whose attainment would be hampered by aggressive regulation" (Kramer & Michalowski, 1991, p. 6). This distinction should serve as a jumping-off point for further classificatory schemes, theory development, and hypothesis testing.

HISTORICAL PERSPECTIVE

There are many historical examples through the dual processes of colonialism and imperialism that, in retrospect, might be labeled state-corporate crimes. They include but are not limited to the genocide of indigenous peoples; the ongoing appropriation of Native American lands; the international slave trade; convict leasing to wealthy land owners in southern states in the United States; the private ownership of everything from the means of production to schools, churches, and stores in mining communities; and the use of armies and the police to contain and in some cases quash labor strikes in England, Canada, and the United States (e.g., Brown & Brown, 1978; Matthiessen, 1991; Taft & Ross, 1979; Tunnell, 1995a, 1995b). Likewise, relatively recent events like the savings and loan crisis (1989) and the *Exxon Valdez* oil spill (1989) appear to have the trappings of state-corporate crime but have not yet been examined through this theoretical lens. The connections between government and corporations have been exposed by the mainstream media, the alternative media, and through the hard work of individuals like Ralph Nader and the numerous organizations that he helped establish.

Contemporary cases that have been explicitly labeled as state-corporate crimes include an analysis of the January 1986 space shuttle explosion; the September 1991 deadly Imperial Chicken processing plant fire in Hamlet, North Carolina; and the U.S. Department of Energy's role in nuclear weapons production (Aulette & Michalowski, 1993; Kauzlarich & Kramer, 1998; Kramer, 1992).

The explosion of the *Challenger* technically resulted from faulty seals; however, a deeper analysis points to the "hurry-up" agenda of the National Aeronautics and Space Administration (NASA), which is a state agency, and the management of Morton Thiokol, the company that manufactured the seals. Although corporate engineers voiced misgivings over the scheduled flight of the shuttle, their concerns were over-ridden by both NASA and Morton Thiokol's management—which yielded to state-corporate pressures to produce a series of space shuttle flights in a set time. The fatal consequences—the death of seven astronauts and the loss of millions of dollars of equipment—were the result of both private producers and state managers whose concerns for production, flight schedules, and a financially self-sufficient space shuttle program overshadowed those for human life (Kramer, 1992; Vaughn, 1996).

In September 1991, an Imperial Chicken processing plant fire in Hamlet, North Carolina, killed 25 people. This is another recent example of the state's omissive behavior while it at the same time engaged in anticipatory policies to encourage corporations to accumulate increasing wealth. In fact, North Carolina's history of regulatory failure by state and federal agencies contributed to the tragedy in Hamlet. North Carolina failed to fund (and to use available federal funds toward) its own State Occupational Safety and Health Program—a program designed to protect workers' safety while on the job. Federal funding for its own Occupational Safety and Health Administration (OSHA) program had decreased in the pro-business, anti-labor political climate of the 1980s in the United States. North Carolina had promoted a social climate friendly to business and hostile to labor and corporate regulation. The state had its own right-to-work laws that weakened the little power organized labor held. Workers at Imperial, paid slightly more than minimum wage, were nonunion and likely would have remained that way (Shanker, 1992).

Regulatory inspectors (i.e., state agents) knew that Imperial kept fire exit doors locked to prevent workers from stealing chicken parts. Because the doors were locked, 25 workers died in the fire. The state, in this case, shirked its responsibilities for protecting workers (which in this case amounts to enforcing the law) and allowed a corporation to engage in illegal and ultimately deadly actions (Aulette & Michalowski, 1993; Wright, Cullen, & Blankenship, 1995). Although the company was fined $800,000 in civil fines (the largest in North Carolina history) for 54 "willful" safety violations and 23 "serious" violations, and the owner of the company was sentenced to prison for manslaughter, the state of North Carolina emerged unblemished. This case is an example of the state playing a role to foster a climate that solicits business and discourages workers from organizing, while failing to protect its citizens against working in a life-threatening environment.

State-corporate crime, such as that in North Carolina, has been facilitated by the recent dominating conservative government and politics in the United States. For example, guarantees of an individual state's rights can be viewed as unchecked power. Relinquishing such power to individual states and provinces while at the same time reducing federal funds available to them for enforcing regulatory law undermines the importance and necessity of worker protection that federal legislation was designed to guarantee.

Kauzlarich and Kramer (1998) apply the concept of state crime to the actions of the U.S. government in three interrelated policy areas: the use and threatened use of nuclear weapons, the production of atomic weapons, and the involuntary and nonconsensual radiation experiments on humans. The authors review many well-known incidents of governmental wrongdoing in the area of nuclear policy and practice.

They argue that "many of the actions that the United States government has taken with regard to nuclear weapons are illegal under international or domestic law, and therefore, a form of state crime" (Kauzlarich & Kramer, 1998, p. 3). Kauzlarich and Kramer outline the International Court of Justice's stance concerning the use of nuclear weapons and the laws of war. They examine the threat underlying the possible use of atomic weapons during the Korean and Vietnam Wars, how the production of nuclear weapons has contaminated the environment, the indignity of human radiation experiments, and finally how to "explain and control the crimes of the nuclear state."

In addition, there has been some analysis of Wedtech defense contractor fraud (Friedrichs, 1996) and the crash of ValuJet flight 592 in May 1996 (Matthews & Kauzlarich, 2000), both of which are placed in the state-corporate crime context. In the former, under the pretense of helping disadvantaged minority businesses, the Small Business Administration, White House aides, a number of congressmen, and then-Attorney General Edwin Meese III were implicated in corruption charges. In the latter, it was discovered that the government inspectors (i.e., the Federal Aviation Administration) who were supposed to inspect the safety operations of ValuJet and Sabre technologies (which had a contract with the airline company) were negligent in their affairs. This omission led to the deaths of all 109 individuals on board when the plane crashed in the Florida Everglades.

It goes without saying that there are countless examples of state-corporate crime that have been committed by U.S. concerns in foreign countries. The chemical explosion at a Union Carbide plant in Bhopal, India (occurring

December 23, 1994) is a case in point (Pearce & Tombs, 1998). As a result of this tragedy, thousands of people (perhaps as many as 4,000) were killed either by the toxic fumes or when they left in terror, and hundreds of thousands were permanently injured (some estimates range as high as 400,000).

CAUSES

When tragedies such as the *Challenger* explosion or the Hamlet, North Carolina, fire occur, or processes whereby the state oversees nuclear production and proliferation, the government holds a unique position. On one hand, the state is established to protect its citizens, and is also the moderator of numerous conflicts that develop in our society, but on the other hand, it is complicitous in the crime. In the problem of state-corporate crime, the state, as coconspirator, continues to exercise its authority in its role as investigator of the crime, prosecutor, and fact-finder/adjudicator (judge) of its own involvement in transgressions. The potential for increasing state-corporate crime activities is stunning and obviously is especially detrimental to people and groups who, compared to corporations and states, possess little power (e.g., workers, poor landowners, subsistence farmers, and indigenous peoples).

According to Parenti (1995),

> On major politico-economic issues, business gets its way with government because there exists no alternative way of organizing investment and production within the existing capitalist structure. Because business controls the very economy of the nation, government perforce enters into a uniquely intimate relationship with it. The health of the economy is treated by policymakers as a necessary condition for the health of the nation, and since it happens that the economy is in the hands of large interests, then presumably government's service to the public is best accomplished by service to these interests. The goals of business (high profits and secure markets) become the goal of government, and the "national interest" becomes identified with the systematic needs of corporate capitalism. (p. 316)

In all three cases, the state had engaged in specific actions in association with the private sector to work toward mutually beneficial material and political objectives. At the same time, the government failed in its obligation to ensure safety as it participated in the creation of a climate that was hostile both to criticism and to specific individuals engaged in progressive politics that were designed to protect the workers' safety.

In the case of the *Challenger,* government managers acted in ways that directly affected the explosion and loss of lives. Their actions were exemplified in the pressure they exerted on the private corporation's engineers. Furthermore, state managers' actions in the executive branch of government pressured NASA's managers to persuade Morton Thiokol's engineers and executives to push on despite doubts. In this state-corporate crime, political officials' actions indict the state in a crime of commission. On the other hand, the Imperial Chicken processing plant fire, another political illegality where people lost their lives, resulted from state agents' inactions or omissions.

The State of North Carolina failed to ensure workers' safety from such dangers in the work place. The state and its agents (viz., North Carolina's OSHA) failed to inspect the hazardous work site; indeed, in the plant's 11 years of operation, it had never been inspected by OSHA. Thus, this state-corporate illegality is best explained by the state's failure to act and is treated as a political crime of omission. It also is a political crime of commission. North Carolina engaged in official and overt policies and practices that culminated in creating an environmental, business, and regulatory climate ripe for just such a tragedy. North Carolina simultaneously attracted low-wage, anti-union businesses and understaffed its own OSHA regulatory agency. The state's official policies and actions contributed to events that resulted in deaths that are best explained as state-corporate crimes of commission and omission.

SUMMARY

This chapter has described a relatively new category of political crime—state-corporate crime. This unique variety of political illegality results from interrelationships between the private and public sectors. These "mutually reinforcing interactions" often result in legal violations that are driven by political and private agendas. The potential for further harms resulting from these relationships is alarming, particularly considering that regulatory law aimed at controlling private corporations is today being scaled back while corporations are increasingly transcending national borders both in production and in advancing the consumption of their products. In effect, controls on such political crimes may offer less protection for workers, consumers, and citizens than they have in the past and particularly in precarious economic times. In addition, the majority of research in this area appears to be in the American context. Clearly, corporations in other countries also collude with government in a criminogenic fashion. Finally, it appears that the majority of state-corporate crimes are crimes of omission. Potential problems are conveniently ignored because they would require an additional outlay of funds, something the corporation or state wants to conserve.

NOTE

1. Perhaps it is also necessary to define what a corporation is. In general, in the eyes of the law, it is treated as a person. It is a joint venture in which incorporation provides the owner better protection against liability. It is a much less risky venture to set up one's business as a corporation than as a sole proprietorship or a limited partnership.

TEST QUESTIONS

Multiple-Choice

1. The concept of state-corporate crime was first applied to which case?
   a. Apollo case
   b. Imperial Chicken case
   c. *Challenger* case
   d. ValuJet 592 case
   e. the Holocaust

2. How many people died in the Imperial Chicken processing plant fire (September 1992)?
   a. 15
   b. 30
   c. 20
   d. 25
   e. 100

3. Who first defined state-corporate crime?
   a. Kramer
   b. Ross
   c. Stewart
   d. Sutherland
   e. Kauzlarich

4. Where did the Imperial Chicken plant fire occur?
   a. Orlando, Florida
   b. Hamlet, North Carolina
   c. Raleigh, North Carolina
   d. St. Marys, Maryland
   e. Imperial, Ohio

5. The explosion of the Space Shuttle *Challenger* resulted from
   a. a fuel leak
   b. pilot error
   c. faulty controls
   d. faulty seals
   e. none of the above

6. Why do individuals, groups, and businesses form corporations?
   a. increase profits
   b. limit liability
   c. tax advantages
   d. all the above
   e. none of the above

7. In what nation did the Bhopal incident take place?
   a. Argentina
   b. Canada
   c. Great Britain
   d. India
   e. United States

Short Answer

1. List three contemporary examples of state-corporate crime reviewed by the book.

2. List and explain the two typologies of state-corporate crime.

3. What is the difference between corporate crime and state-corporate crime?

4. Why does it appear that the majority of state-corporate crimes are crimes of omission?

⊰ TWELVE ⊱

CONCLUSION

Controlling Oppositional and State Crime

———•◦•———

This book's central perspective is that political crime is an important subject deserving investigation and explanation, and that a complete understanding can be achieved only when one appreciates the definitional issues, history, causes, and effects, is current, integrates cases, understands theory, and presents and evaluates relevant policy and practices. Inevitably, we must deal with the thorny issue of control. Compared to scholars of most types of crime, those of political crime do not offer much advice on minimizing this phenomenon (Barkan, 2001): "Part of this reason is that the political crime literature is relatively scant to begin with. Another reason is that political crime is so universal, both historically and cross-nationally, that it almost seems natural and inevitable" (p. 393). Barkan suggests, "If as I've argued, political crime is best understood as a function of power, then to reduce political crime we must reduce the disparities of power that characterize many societies. At a minimum, this means moving from authoritarian to democratic rule." Although Barkan has a good point, the countries that we've examined are noted for being the world's most prominent democracies, yet they still have political crime. He notes,

> The historical record also indicates that dissenters will turn to civil disobedience and other illegal activities as long as they perceive flawed governmental policies. One way to reduce some political crime, then, would be to reduce

poverty, racial discrimination, military adventurism, and other conditions and policies that promote humanitarian dissent. . . . At a minimum, responsible political officials from all sides of the political spectrum must state in no uncertain terms their opposition to these inhumane forms of dissent. (Barkan, 2001, p. 394)

Perhaps through explanation and responsible control measures we might help create a society that is both more compassionate and based on human and social justice.

This chapter examines the issue of controlling political crime. Short of eliminating the state (e.g., Martin, 1995), individuals, organizations, and states have used a variety of methods to combat, eliminate, minimize, reduce, or simply control anti-systemic and state crime. Research and practice to date reveal a series of methods previously used to control both oppositional and state crimes. These techniques are reviewed and critiqued.

Admittedly, the strategies offered here are not exhaustive and in some instances are not very concrete. Because there is such wide variance among advanced industrialized countries and the types of crimes that occur therein, these methods are best understood if presented as suggestions for controlling political crime. Also, it must be noted that strategies for controlling political crimes by or against particular capitalist states may not be subject to generalization to others.

Particular cultures and the organization of state structures play significant roles in giving rise to specific methods for controlling political crime. Undoubtedly, there are similarities in controlling political illegalities that cut across states that share similar economies and political systems, as is the case with advanced, industrialized, capitalist, democratic states. One also must be mindful that traditional controls on oppositional crimes have often resulted in state crimes!

Controls are exercised by a variety of individuals and from a number of institutions characteristic of democratic societies. Most of these organizations have the typical constraints found in bureaucratic organizations. Regardless of the state agency, we can probably divide the controls into two types: internal and external. Internal controls include such mechanisms as supervisors and chains of command. External controls can be classified as governmental/ legislative solutions or nongovernmental/citizen ones. Control in advanced industrialized democracies is typically exercised through a combination of internal and external mechanisms.

CONTROLLING OPPOSITIONAL CRIME

Although not willing to use the term *state crime,* Turk (1982a, chap. 4), in his discussion of political policing, outlines five controls (including those concerned with maintaining national and public security) used by the police in their capacity of political policing: intelligence, information control, neutralization (specific deterrence), intimidation (general deterrence), and statecraft. Despite Turk's sophisticated and articulate analysis, relationships among these influences remain untested.

Even though framed in terms of responses to dissent in Eastern European countries, Braun's (1989, p. 118) outline of five state approaches to dissent can equally be applied to the advanced industrialized countries—incapacitation, deterrence (including general and individual), co-optation, containment, and coexistence—and she suggests that they may be "incorporated" into broader strategies of dealing with dissent, which she identifies as pacification through partial inclusion, repressive tolerance, differentiated political justice, and suppression through force. As with earlier attempts, however, the interconnectedness of state responses to political crimes is not articulated. Nevertheless, I believe the best strategy integrates the less objectionable features of both Turk's and Braun's categories[1] and draws connections among them in an attempt to provide a more informed, responsible, and progressive approach for controlling anti-systemic political crime. These categories are consolidated into five types and listed from least to most utilized by state agents. This rendering, however, is not an endorsement of these strategies.

First, *inclusion* occurs when the state and elites involve political dissenters by offering them positions in the public administration or a political party. This often quells the more unsavory types of opposition by making them part of the political and economic system. They are treated to the perks and privileges that positions like this afford.

Second, *responsible policing* represents the use of legal methods to temporarily terminate the activities of people and organizations that engage in so-called political crimes.

Third, *deterrence* (including general and specific) would include Turk's (1982a) potentially objectionable categories of neutralization and intimidation. Here, "The aim is to neutralize resistance in ways that ensure that offenders will not repeat (specific deterrence), and [that] contribute to inhibiting any

---

Box 12.1   Noam Chomsky (December 7, 1928-)

Born in Philadelphia Pennsylvania, Chomsky is Professor of Linguistics at the Massachusetts Institute of Technology in Cambridge, Massachusetts. Although he started his academic career as a linguist and has achieved distinction in this field (especially because of his books *Syntactic Structures* [1957] and *Aspects of the Theory of Syntax* [1965]), he is perhaps better known as a leading intellectual, analyst of power, and one of the most outspoken critics of U.S. foreign policy and the elite media.

Chomsky is the author of numerous articles and books, including *American Power and the New Mandarins* (1969), *Radical Priorities* (1981), *The Fateful Triangle* (1983), *Pirates & Emperors* (1987), *Manufacturing Consent* (1988) (with Edward Herman), and *Deterring Democracy* (1991). He is a frequent contributor to left liberal and anarchist publications and a speaker at activist functions. He is often interviewed by the alternative press, and his speeches are broadcast on Amy Goodman's "Democracy Now" show, which is aired on Pacifica Radio. He is the subject of a handful of books (e.g., Milan Rai's *Chomsky's Politics* (1995) that analyze his politics.

---

inclinations others may have to resist the authorities (general deterrence)" (p. 137). According to Turk, one of the ways to accomplish this is through terror and the other is through enclosure. People "may acquiesce out of fear and ignorance. . . . General deterrence is the ultimate goal of political policing; it is the anticipated product of intimidation" (p. 150). The challenge here is to implement these goals in a just fashion.

Fourth, a variety of government departments use legal *intelligence methods* to "detect potential as well as actual resistance. The more threatened they feel, the greater will be the effort to monitor thoughts and feelings as well as behavior and relationships" (Turk, 1982a, p. 123). Intelligence gathering not only allows authorities to keep abreast of threats to the regime or of political criminality.

Finally, *statecraft* is

> the art and science of social control as developed and used in the political
> organization of social life. Narrowly construed as the operations of political
> police, political policing may be understood as just the sharpest cutting edge
> of a more encompassing multidimensional effort to accomplish political
> dominance. More broadly construed as the total process by which intolerable
> political opposition is prevented as well as punished, political policing finally
> becomes synonymous with government. (Turk, 1982a, p. 160)

Turk, building on Gamson (1968), outlines three ways authorities can
prohibit political resistance: insulation, sanctions, and persuasion. He distinguishes between internal and foreign control and also examines the problem
of unintended consequences from controlling oppositional political crimes.
For instance, "internal control . . . does not itself constitute a solution to the
problems created by nature or external social influences" (Turk, 1982a,
p. 173).

In many countries,

> the reduction or elimination of ordinary legal restraints in dealing with polit-
> ical criminality has been accomplished partly by direct legislation and judi-
> cial decision, but largely and more effectively by the creation and operation
> of special investigative and quasi-judicial bodies . . . as well as various coun-
> terinsurgency "intelligence" agencies and programs. Some of the extraordi-
> nary measures which have been authorized by the Congress, and generally
> supported by the courts are: restriction of the right to travel, both outside
> and within the country; limitation of the right to seek and hold employment,
> governmental and nongovernmental; electronic and nonelectronic surveillance
> on a "possibly relevant" instead of a "probable cause" basis; compulsory
> disclosure of self-incriminating evidence; and denial of access to trial courts.
> It should be noted that such legislation has typically undergone some delim-
> itation in the judicial process, and has in rare cases ultimately been found
> unconstitutional. (Turk, 1982a, pp. 64-65)[2]

CONTROLLING STATE CRIME

Controlling state crime is difficult because much of the government's illegalities are hidden from the public, including the media (Barak, 1990, p. 15;
Grabosky, 1989; Ross, 1995/2000). Governments and states conceal their
deviant behaviors as prudent measures to prevent public and media scrutiny

that would otherwise lead to their downfall. Even when the state has engaged in universally despicable behavior, it usually does not admit its wrongdoing but dismisses its activities as necessary for sustaining order. Because the state typically refuses to participate in a critical dialogue or investigation of its misdeeds, there usually is no official recognition of a crime.

Moreover, when confronted with state transgressions, the public has difficulty constructing informed opinions about them because, typically, media news propagates a state-sanctioned consensus (Chomsky, 1988) and maintains the assumption that government officials are trustworthy and capable of leading (e.g., Clinard & Quinney, 1978). Critical queries are rarely heard except in alternative news sources, which lack both a sizeable audience and widespread public acceptance.

Ample documentation exists about the biased nature of mainstream news reporting in many capitalist states. The media saturate consumers with sensationalized, violent street crimes and rarely touch either corporate or government illegality (e.g., Ferrell & Sanders, 1995; Tunnell, 1992). The media's focus on personal crimes also keeps news consumers' attention fixed on street criminals, rather than on state managers' misdeeds (e.g., Reiman, 1998; Warr, 1995).

Consequently, crimes of all varieties by the powerful typically get little attention, and citizens of capitalist states continue to believe that grave threats to them come from individual predators rather than official governmental policies and practices. As a result, state actions go unquestioned because citizens believe that deviants are individual law-violators, rather than government managers and their policies.

A limitation to monitoring and controlling state crime is the strength of a person's point of view. Whether this is philosophically or ideologically based, once individuals have adopted or committed themselves to a controversial position, it is often difficult for them to consider information that contradicts their firmly held beliefs. Those who have a blind commitment to the government (perhaps superpatriots) will say it was not a state crime. Unwavering adherence to an ideology can prevent individuals from paying attention to subtle nuances (e.g., the Nuremberg Trials).

Apathy, an immense barrier to combating state crimes, often results from state harms being ignored or perhaps dismissed by public or private interests (Ross, 2000b, chap. 5). Given the state's contradictory involvement as both offender and dispenser of justice, victims of state crime rarely are compensated or satisfied (Barak, 1991). In order for victims to receive some type of justice, the government must first recognize that its agents and policies are socially harmful.

Nevertheless, there are various methods for controlling state crimes. Some researchers present a list of factors important in the control of particular state criminogenic institutions or state crimes.[3] Moreover, other theorists have outlined a series of responses, if not controls for state crime. Although brought up in the context of state repression in the United States, Wolfe (1973) suggested that the adoption of socialism would lead to a cessation of state crimes. Unfortunately, he did not consider the historical examples where, during the practice of socialism in a number of Western European countries and Israel, the state committed numerous crimes against its citizens (Ross, 2000c). Grabosky's (1989) tentative theory of state crime, for example, is accompanied by six basic outcomes of state crime: "deterrence," "rehabilitation," "victim compensation," "denouncing the misconduct in question," "reaffirming the rule of law," and "experienc[ing] the threat (or reality) of draconian punishment" (pp. 17-18, 303-308).

Basing his work on the understanding that, given the diversity of official misconduct, there can be no one intervention or control answering the problem, Grabosky (1989) includes seven methods of controlling state crime: "internal oversight," "organizational redesign," "external oversight," "whistle blowing," "criminal prosecution," "civil litigation," and "participatory democracy" (pp. 308-331).[4] His work is an important starting point in the academic effort to understand the control of state crime and to prevent the abuse, and to secure the proper use of state power.[5] Similarly, Kauzlarich and Kramer (1998) construct an organizational model of the causes and control of state crime that needs to be expanded and integrated.

Before making suggestions, let me outline what does not work. Usually, changes that are symbolic in nature have no effect. They are simply palliative and may in fact contribute to increased dissent. Some of the more popular, relatively low-cost and ineffective sleights of hand have been name changes and/or the recruiting of new directors or administrators who have minimal experience or power. Rarely do they have the ability to change the pervasive effects of organizational culture.

Ross (1995/2000, chap. 1), on the other hand, develops a structural model of control that helps minimize the amount, frequency, and intensity of state crime. The model outlines the principal state criminogenic actors and the main actors that exist to control state crimes, including victims' methods of controlling state crime; controls in context; and internal (state controlled) and external (both state and nonstate controlled) mechanisms for combating state crimes. Although Ross specifies a series of propositions for testing, suggestions for data collection and testing have not been formulated. In the meantime, there are six

BOX 12.2   Peter Grabosky (1941-)

Trained as a political scientist, Peter Grabosky works for the Regulatory Institutions Network at the Australian National University in Canberra. He has written a considerable number of articles and books on crime and politics. His best-known books include *The Politics of Crime and Conflict: A Comparative History of Four Cities* (1977) (with Ted Robert Gurr & Richard C. Hula); *Sydney in Ferment: Crime, Dissent, and Official Reaction, 1788-1973* (1977); and *Wayward Governance: Illegality and Its Control in the Public Sector* (1989). He is also the co-author of *Electronic Theft: Unlawful Acquisition in Cyberspace* (2001) and *Crime in the Digital Age: Controlling Telecommunications and Cyberspace Illegalities* (1998). He was born in the United States and later moved to Australia, where he was deputy director of the Australian Institute of Criminology. In July 1998, he was elected president of the Australian and New Zealand Society of Criminology and the following year was elected to the board of directors, and was deputy secretary-general of the International Society of Criminology. Grabosky's general interests are in the prevention and control of computer-related crime.

principal methods to control state crime in advanced industrialized countries that should be maintained, if not given additional attention. They are listed from least to most important.

First, an important control is *the development, consultation, and reliance on ethics departments in government.* Many state agencies at the federal, state, and local levels in advanced industrialized countries have departments or units that not only provide some form of internal oversight, but help to educate and monitor their employees regarding appropriate ethics. To buttress this control, many departments have a unit often called an inspector general to investigate real or alleged abuses and to recommend appropriate sanctions. In addition, whistleblower legislation, which allows employees immunity from prosecution if they reveal government illegalities and mismanagement, is present in many but not all levels of government.

Second, *empowering victims:* This involves the socialization, education, and training of individuals who may be subject to government abuse so they can voice their concerns to the proper audiences. It also means the development of an infrastructure to protect victims and to educate victimizers about the distasteful nature of their deeds. A focus on victims also allows us to reward political whistleblowers when appropriate.

Third, *using the free market economic system:* This implies that the power of money is extremely relevant to the process of controlling state crime. People and organizations can boycott companies that do business in countries that engage in state crimes, and they can lobby their representatives to pass legislation that enforces trade controls on items that mitigate workers' rights. Recently, workers and activists suggested that to control these types of crime, countries should tightly control trade by banning products manufactured by corporations that are unfair to workers, that use child labor, and that have little regard for the environment (e.g., Greider, 1992). Such strategies are being implemented today and represent starting points for controlling this type of state crime against labor (Tunnell, 1995a).

Fourth, *fielding social justice candidates in elections:* This is another method for working within the existing democratic system to publicize policies that keep state criminogenic agencies in check. This means that major and fringe parties would run candidates and that independents would be willing to voice opposition to state policies that are socially harmful and that represent human rights violations.

Fifth, *using the courts:* The democratic freedoms that are constitutionally given could be better protected while minimizing attempts to withdraw those privileges. However, the courts in capitalist states undoubtedly play a significant part in preserving order, enforcing the will of the government, limiting the activities of labor, and adjudicating conflicts between the state and labor. Most democracies have well-thought-out procedures that specify how public officials can be kicked out of office. In the United Sates, for example, the right to impeach public officials is outlined by the U.S. Constitution in Article I, Sections 2 and 3, which discuss the procedure, and in Article II, Section 4, which indicates the grounds for impeachment: "the President, Vice President, and all civil officers of the United States shall be removed from office on Impeachment for, and Conviction of Treason, Bribery, or other high Crimes and Misdemeanors."

Sixth, and most important, is *strong external oversight:* This includes agencies that can monitor the wrongdoing of government agencies and personnel. It also involves the proper selection of managers and their training in techniques to monitor the work of their employees. This includes watchdog agencies, special prosecutors (with circumscribed powers), and/or an effective system of checks and balances. There will always be flaws in any possible or implemented solution; monitoring state crime is therefore an ongoing reality. One response might be to have more people on the inside, like integrity officers, to be on the lookout for crimes. Perhaps sanctions for state employees need to be harsher?

Pessimism abounds on both ideological and structural grounds regarding the possibility of controlling the state (Barak, 2000; Ross, 1995/2000, 2000c). Although proposing solutions is easy, those that are realistic and practical for minimizing political crime are far from simple. Yet, these crimes are the ones that—due to their far-reaching effects—most need to be controlled.

Chances are that as long as states exist, there will always be crime committed by government actors. However, most of those caught receive light sanctions because of the resources they have or can get access to. Like the old philosophical question, "If a tree falls in the forest but no one hears it, did it make a sound?", in order for a crime to have occurred, someone or some agency needs to know that an illegality has been committed. Governments are adept at concealing their actions. In addition, state crime occurs at all levels of government and is widespread, so monitoring and controlling it is extremely difficult. The state has a disproportionate amount of resources, including money and personnel. Typical monitoring entities may be influenced to look the other way or actively participate in the cover-up. With any type of social problem or crime, there is no absolute or concrete solution. People must become increasingly intolerant of state misconduct, overt and covert, rather than expect a solution from the state. In addition, incentives must be given to government workers to "snitch" on other workers who commit abuses. Stricter checks and balances must be put into place. If you have the power to commit a state crime, generally you have the power to shift the blame.

In short, a number of traditional and innovative controls have been implemented to minimize, reduce, control, or prevent these types of crimes from occurring again. Determining which ones work in what situations is important. Having the will and resources to experiment with new solutions is probably the only way we can develop a more just society.

SUMMARY AND CONCLUSION

Although some may question whether it is realistic to control oppositional and state crime simultaneously, we need to be reminded that when the government tries to prevent or minimize threats to its existence, this needs to be done without violating the law. Otherwise the state would be using a double standard, something the general public would find morally and ethically puzzling.

Political crime will exist as long as the entity we call "the state" exists. In the future, the center of political power may very well shift temporarily or permanently to transnational corporations and organizations. The question remaining is whether in the future political crime will increase or decrease. The answer depends on reasoned analysis. What we do know, however, is that most anti-systemic political crime is a barometer of citizens' discontent with their government (elected or appointed), including the public administration (bureaucracy). State crime, on the other hand, is too often an indicator of incompetence, lack of training, competition among organizational units, lack of coordination, and overall paranoia on the part of well-placed bureaucrats.

Although human rights violations and state violence (perhaps with the exception of police use of excessive force) are relatively rare in advanced industrialized democracies, state-corporate crime and terrorism should persist and may increase. Especially because of the attacks on the Pentagon and the World Trade Center on September 11, 2001, Americans are more cautious and feel more vulnerable to being victimized by terrorism.

Perhaps, when the history of our decade is written, we will look back and point to a number of incidents of state repression instituted in the wake of "September 11th" or as a result of the U.S. Patriot Act passed in the aftermath of the World Trade Center and Pentagon attacks. As long as there are states and power differentials, political crime will exist.

NOTES

1. The meaning of Braun's categories is inferred where appropriate.

2. Turk (1982a) warns that there are changes afoot with respect to monitoring dissent, particularly these: "in the Western democracies: (1) increasing use of field controls, (2) expanding surveillance coupled with more selective targeting for neutralization, (3) more 'subcontracting' of operations, and (4) the internationalization of control policies and programs" (p. 199).

3. See Ross (1995a) for a review of this literature.

4. Although Grabosky has sensitized us to the need for more analytical techniques, his factors have received criticism (e.g., Ross, 1995/2000, p. 9).

5. Grabosky (1989) outlines a series of reasons why studying state crime is important that can be applied in this situation too, including, "breaches of the law by governments can entail very great cost, in financial as well as in human terms"; "personal embarrassment" of elected officials and governments; violations of rights; and "attacks on the rule of law" (p. 4).

TEST QUESTIONS

Multiple-Choice

1. Who developed the only tentative theory of state crime?
    a. Grabosky
    b. Gurr
    c. Marx
    d. Barak
    e. Ziegler

2. To which countries did Braun apply her research?
    a. Anglo American democracies
    b. Eastern European countries
    c. advanced industrialized countries
    d. North American countries
    e. Asian countries

3. Co-option is most favorable with
    a. young dissenters
    b. old dissenters
    c. foreigners
    d. all of the above
    e. none of the above

4. According to Turk, statecraft is
    a. employing intelligence
    b. marshalling resources
    c. to be avoided at all costs
    d. used by oppositional political terrorists
    e. the art and science of social control

5. How many outcomes does Grabosky's tentative theory of state crime have?
    a. 4
    b. 5
    c. 7
    d. 10
    e. 12

6. What is one method of using the free market economic system to control state crime?
    a. creating a technology corridor
    b. using lotteries
    c. selling products at higher prices
    d. boycotting
    e. none of the above

7. In the future should there be more or less state crime?
    a. more state crime
    b. less state crime
    c. as long as states exist there will be political crime
    d. it will increase and decrease
    e. none of the above

Short Answer

1. What are four controls on state crime?

2. What are Turk's five controls, listed in the context of political policing?

3. What are three ways authorities can prohibit political resistance?

4. Is it realistic to attempt to control oppositional political crimes and state crimes at the same time?

REFERENCES

About. (2002). *Human Rights Watch.* Retrieved June 8, 2002, from http://www. hrw.org/about/about.html

Ackroyd, C., Margolis, K., Rosenhead, J., & Shalice, T. (1980). *The technology of political control* (2nd ed.). London: Pluto Press.

Ackroyd, P. (2001). *London: The biography.* New York: Doubleday.

Agee, P. (1975). *Inside the Company: CIA diary.* New York: Routledge.

Akehurst, M. (1987). *Introduction to international law.* London: Unwin Hyman.

Akers, R. L. (1994). *Criminological theories: Introduction and evaluation.* Los Angeles: Roxbury.

Alexander, D. W. (1992a). *Applying Merton's theory of anomie to political criminality.* Paper presented to the American Society of Criminology annual meetings, New Orleans.

Alexander, D. W. (1992b). *Political crime: An application of Merton's theory of social structure and anomie.* Master's thesis, Virginia Polytechnic Institute and State University.

Alford, R., & Friedland, R. (1985). *Powers of theory: Capitalism, the state, and democracy.* New York: Cambridge University Press.

Alford, R., & Friedland, R. (1986). *Powers of theory.* Cambridge, UK: Cambridge University Press.

Allen, F. A. (1974). *The crime of politics: Political dimensions of criminal justice.* Cambridge, MA: Harvard University Press.

Amnesty International. (2002). Retrieved June 8, 2002, from http://www.amnesty.org/

Archer, J. (1971*). Treason in America: Disloyalty versus dissent.* New York: Hawthorn.

Aulette, J. R., & Michalowski, R. (1993). Fire in Hamlet: A case study of state-corporate crime. In Kenneth D. Tunnell (Ed.), *Political crime in contemporary America: A critical approach* (pp. 171-206). New York: Garland.

Bachrach, P., & Baratz, M. S. (1962). Two faces of power. *American Political Science Review, 56,* 947-952.

Balagopal, K. (1986). Deaths in police custody: Whom and why do the police kill? *Economic and Political Weekly, 21,* 2028-2029.

Balbus, I. (1977). *The dynamics of legal repression.* New York: Transaction Books.

Barak, G. (1990). Crime, criminology and human rights: Towards an understanding of state criminality. *Journal of Human Justice, 2*(1), 11-28.

Barak, G. (Ed.). (1991). *Crimes by the capitalist state: An introduction to state criminality*. Albany: State University of New York Press.

Barak, G. (1993). Crime, criminology, and human rights: Toward an understanding of state criminality. In K. D. Tunnell (Ed.), *Political crime in contemporary America* (pp. 207-230). New York: Garland.

Barak, G. (Ed.). (1994). *Media, process, and the social construction of crime: Studies in newsmaking criminology*. New York: Garland.

Barak, G. (Ed.). (1996). *Representing O.J.: Murder, criminal justice, and mass culture*. Albany, NY: Harrow and Heston.

Barak, G. (2000). Preface. In J. I. Ross (Ed.), *Varieties of state crime and its control* (pp. vii-ix). Monsey, NY: Criminal Justice Press.

Barkan, S. (2001). *Criminology: A sociological understanding* (2nd ed.). Upper Saddle River, NJ: Prentice Hall.

Barlow, H. D., & Kauzlarich, D. (2002). *Introduction to criminology* (8th ed.). Upper Saddle River, NJ: Prentice Hall.

Beirne, P., & Messerschmidt, J. (1991). *Criminology*. New York: Harcourt Brace Jovanovich.

Bell, J. B. (1978). *A time of terror*. New York: Basic Books.

Bell, J. B., & Gurr, T. R. (1979). Terrorism and revolution in America. In H. D. Graham & T. R. Gurr (Eds.), *Violence in America* (pp. 329-347). Beverly Hills, CA: Sage.

Bennett, A. L. (1991). *International organizations: Principles and issues* (5th ed.). Englewood Cliffs, NJ: Prentice Hall.

Benyon, J. (1984). *Scarman and after: Essays reflecting on Lord Scarman's report, the riots and their aftermath*. Elmsford, NY: Pergamon.

Berman, M. R., & Clark, R. S. (1982). State terrorism: Disappearances. *Rutgers Law Journal, 13*, 531-577.

Bernheim, J.-C. (1990). *Police et pouvoir d'homicide*. Montreal: Meridien.

Binder, A., & Fridell, L. (1984, June). Lethal force as a police response. *Criminal Justice Abstracts*, pp. 256-280.

Binder, A., & Scharf, P. (1980). The violent police-citizen encounter. *Annals of the American Academy of Political and Social Science, 452*, 111-121.

Black's law dictionary. (1994). (6th ed., p. 1335). New York: Kluwer Academic.

Blackstock, N. (1975). *The FBI's secret war against political freedom*. New York: Vintage.

Block, F. (1977). The ruling class does not rule. *Socialist Revolution, 33*, 18-31.

Blumberg, M. (1982). *The use of firearms by police officers: The impact of individuals, communities and race*. Unpublished doctoral dissertation, State University of New York, Albany.

Bodansky, Y. (2001). *Bin Laden: The man who declared war on America*. Roseville, CA: Prima Publishing.

Bohm, R. M. (1982). Radical criminology: An explication. *Criminology, 19*, 565-589.

Bohm, R. M. (1993). Social relationships that arguably should be criminal although they are not: On the political economy of crime. In K. D. Tunnell (Ed.), *Political crime in contemporary America* (pp. 2-29). New York: Garland.

Bollinger, L. (1981). Die Entwicklung zu terroristischem Handeln als psychosozialer Prozess: Begegnungen mit Beteiligten. In H. Jager, G. Schmidtchen, & L. Süllwold (Eds.), *Analysen zum Terrorismus* (Vol. 2). Oplanden, Germany: Westdeutscher Verlag.

Borovoy, A. (1985). Freedom of expression: Some recurring impediments. In R. Abella & M. L. Rothman (Eds.), *Justice beyond Orwell* (pp. 125-160). Montreal: Les Editions Yvon Blais.

Box, S. (1983). *Power, crime, and mystification*. London: Tavistock.

Boyle, A. (1979). *The climate of treason: Five who spied for Russia*. London: Hutchinson.

Braun, A. (1989). Dissent and the state in Eastern Europe. In C. E. S. Franks (Ed.), *Dissent and the state* (pp. 111-137). Toronto: Oxford University Press.

Brown, L., & Brown, C. (1978). *An unauthorized history of the RCMP.* Toronto: James Lorimer.

Brown, M. F. (1984). Use of deadly force by patrol officers—Training implementation. *Journal of Police Science and Administration, 12,* 133-140.

Bryan, G. S. (1943). *The spy in America*. Philadelphia: J. B. Lippincott.

Bunyan, T. (1976). *The political police in Britain*. New York: St. Martin's.

Burgess, R. L., & Akers, R. L. (1968). A differential association-reinforcement theory of criminal behavior. *Social Problems, 14,* 128-147.

Burnham, D. (1989). *A law unto itself: The IRS and the abuse of power.* New York: Vintage.

Canada. (1981a). *Commission of Inquiry Concerning Certain Activities of the Royal Canadian Mounted Police (the McDonald Commission). Freedom and Security Under the Law*, Second Report. Ottawa: Minster of Supply and Services.

Canada. (1981b). Ministere de la Justice. *Rapport de la commission d'enquete sur des operations policieres en territoire Quebecois* (the Keable Commission).

Canada. (1986a). *Crimes against the state*. Law Reform Commission of Canada, Working Paper 40. (Available from Law Reform Commission of Canada, 130 Albert St. 7th Floor, Ottawa, Ontario. K1A 0L6)

Canada. (1986b). *Crimes against the state*. Law Reform Commission of Canada, Working Paper 49. (Available from Law Reform Commission of Canada, 130 Albert St. 7th Floor, Ottawa, Ontario. K1A 0L6)

Caplan, G. (1983). On Kelman's incorrect conclusions. *American Psychologist, 38,* 1124-1126.

Carnoy, M. (1984). *The state and political theory*. Princeton, NJ: Princeton University Press.

Center for Research on Criminal Justice. (1977). *The iron fist and the velvet glove*. Berkeley, CA: Author.

Chambliss, W. J. (1976). The state and criminal law. In W. J. Chambliss & M. Mankoff (Eds.), *Whose law, what order?* (pp. 66-106). New York: John Wiley.

THE DYNAMICS OF POLITICAL CRIME

Chambliss, W. J., & Seidman, R. (1982). *Law, order, and power* (2nd ed.). Reading, MA: Addison-Wesley.

Chapin, B. (1964). *The American law of treason*. Seattle: University of Washington Press.

Chevigny, P. (1990, June). *Deadly force as social control in the Americas: Jamaica, Brazil, and Argentina*. A paper presented at the Annual Meeting of the Law and Society Association, Madison, WI.

China expels convicted U.S. "spy." (2001). Retrieved July 26, 2001, from http://www.cnn.com/2001/WORLD/asiapcf/east/07/25/china.lishaomin/index.html

Chomsky, N. (1973). *For reasons of state*. New York: Pantheon.

Chomsky, N. (1983). *The fateful triangle*. Boston: South End.

Chomsky, N. (1988). *Manufacturing consent: The political economy of the mass media*. New York: Pantheon.

Christie, N. (1993). *Crime control as industry*. New York: Routledge.

Churchill, W. (1997). *A little matter of genocide: Holocaust and denial in the Americas, 1492 to the present*. San Francisco: City Lights.

Churchill, W., & Vander Wall, J. (1988). *Agents of repression: The FBI's secret wars against the Black Panther Party and the American Indian Movement*. Boston: South End.

Churchill, W., & Vander Wall, J. (1990). *The COINTELPRO papers: Documents from the FBI's secret wars against domestic dissent*. Boston: South End.

CIA's Mail Intercept: Commission on CIA Activities Within the United States. (1978). In M. D. Ermann & R. J. Lundman (Eds.), *Corporate and governmental deviance* (pp. 174-185). New York: Oxford University Press.

Clark, R. P. (1983). Patterns in the lives of ETA members. *Terrorism: An International Journal, 6,* 423-454.

Clarke, R. (1992). *Situational crime prevention: Successful case studies*. Albany, NY: Harrow and Heston.

Clinard, M. B., & Quinney, R. (1978). Crime by government. In M. D. Ermann & R. J. Lundman (Eds.), *Corporate and governmental deviance* (pp. 137-150). New York: Oxford University Press.

Cohen, S. (1993). Human rights and the crimes of the state: The culture of denial. *Australian and New Zealand Journal of Criminology, 26,* 97-115.

Coleman, J. W. (1985). *The criminal elite*. New York: St. Martin's.

Coleman, J. W. (1994). *The criminal elite* (3rd ed.). New York: St. Martin's.

Coleman, J. W. (1995). Respectable crime. In J. F. Sheley (Ed.), *Criminology* (2nd ed., pp. 249-273). Belmont, CA: Wadsworth.

Cooper, H. H. A. (1977). What is a terrorist? A psychological perspective. *Legal Medical Quarterly* (1), 16-32.

Cornell, J. (1969). *The trial of Ezra Pound: A documented account of the treason case by the defendant's lawyer*. New York: John Day.

Corrado, R. R. (1981). A critique of the mental disorder perspective of political terrorism. *International Journal of Law and Psychiatry, 4,* 1-17.

Corrado, R. R., & Davies, G. (2000). Controlling state crime in Canada. In J. I. Ross (Ed.), *Varieties of state crime and its control* (pp. 59-88). Monsey, NY: Criminal Justice Press.

Corrado, R. R., Olivero, A., & Lauderdale, P. (1992). Political deviance. In V. F. Sacco (Ed.), *Deviance: Conformity and control in Canadian society.* Scarborough, Ontario: Prentice Hall.

Correctional Services of Canada. (1992). Violence and suicide in Canadian institutions. *Forum on Corrections Research, 4*(3), 3-5.

Coulter, J., Miller, S., & Walker, M. (1984). *State of siege: Miner's strike 1984.* London: Canary Press.

Cowell, J., & Young, J. (1982). *Policing the riots.* London: Junction Books.

Crayton, J. W. (1983). Terrorism and the psychology of the self. In L. Z. Freedman & Y. Alexander (Eds.), *Perspectives on terrorism* (pp. 33-41). Wilmington, DE: Scholarly Resources.

Crenshaw, M. (1981). The causes of terrorism. *Comparative Politics, 13,* 379-399.

Crenshaw, M. (1985). An organizational approach to the analysis of political terrorism. *Orbis, 4,* 465-489.

Crenshaw, M. (1990a). The logic of terrorism: Terrorist behavior as a product of strategic choice. In W. Reich (Ed.), *Origins of terrorism* (pp. 7-24). Cambridge: Cambridge University Press.

Crenshaw, M. (1990b). Questions to be answered, research to be done, knowledge to be applied. In W. Reich (Ed.), *Origins of terrorism* (pp. 247-260). Cambridge: Cambridge University Press.

Crenshaw, M. (1991). How terrorism declines. *Terrorism and Political Violence, 3*(1), 69-87.

Cullen, F., Maakestad, W., & Cavender, G. (1987). *Corporate crime under attack: The Ford Pinto case and beyond.* Cincinnati, OH: Anderson.

Dahl, R. (1961). *Who governs?* New Haven, CT: Yale University Press.

Daraki-Mallet, M. (1976). *The ESA men.* Athens: Kendros.

Davis, J. K. (1992). *Spying on America: The FBI's Domestic Counterintelligence Program.* New York: Praeger.

Dion, R. (1982). *Crimes of the secret police.* Montreal: Black Rose Books.

Dionne, E. J. (1991). *Why Americans hate politics.* New York: Touchstone Books.

Domhoff, G. W. (1983). *Who rules America now?* New York: Simon and Schuster.

Donner, F. J. (1990). *Protectors of privilege: Red squads and police repression in urban America.* Berkeley: University of California Press.

Earley, P. (1988). *Family of spies: Inside the John Walker spy ring.* New York: Bantam.

Earley, P. (1998). *Confessions of a spy: The real story of Aldrich Ames.* New York: Berkeley Publishing Group.

Ellis, M. (1994). J. Edgar Hoover and the "red summer" of 1919. *Journal of American Studies, 28,* 39-59.

Engels, F. (1942). *The origin of the family, private property and the state.* New York: International Publishers.

Etzioni-Halevy, E. (1989). *Fragile democracy: The use and abuse of power in Western societies.* New Brunswick, NJ: Transaction Publishers.

Evans, P. B., Rueschemeyer, D., & Skocpol, T. (Eds.). *Bringing the state back in.* Cambridge, UK: Cambridge University Press.

Faucher, P., & Fitzgibbins, K. (1989). Dissent and the state in Latin America. In
    C. E. S. Franks (Ed.), *Dissent and the state* (pp. 138-168). Don Mills, Ontario:
    Oxford University Press.
Feld, B. C. (1971). Police violence and protest. *Minnesota Law Review, 55,* 731-778.
Ferracuti, F. (1982). A sociopsychiatric interpretation of terrorism. *Annals of the
    American Academy of Political and Social Science, 463,* 129-140.
Ferracuti, F., & Bruno, F. (1981). Psychiatric aspects of terrorism in Italy. In
    I. L. Barak-Glanmtz & C. R. Huff (Eds.), *The mad, the bad and the different:
    Essays in honor of Simon Dinitz* (pp. 199-213). Lexington, MA: Lexington Books.
Ferrell, J. (1998). Stumbling toward a critical criminology (and into the anarchy and
    imagery of postmodernism. In J. I. Ross (Ed.), *Cutting the edge: Current perspec-
    tives on radical/critical criminology and criminal justice* (pp. 63-76). Westport, CT:
    Praeger.
Ferrell J., & Sanders, C. (Eds.). (1995). *Cultural criminology*. Boston: Northeastern
    University Press.
Fine, R., & Millar, R. (Eds.). (1985). *Policing the miner's strike*. London: Cobden Trust.
Flexner, S., & Flexner, D. (2000). *The pessimist's guide to history: An irresistible com-
    pendium of catastrophes, barbarities, massacres*. New York: HarperPerennial.
Foerstel, H. N. (1997). *Free expression and censorship in America*. Westport, CT:
    Greenwood.
Foerstel, H. N. (1998). *Banned in the media*. Westport, CT: Greenwood.
Forcese, D. P. (1992). *Policing Canadian society*. Scarborough, Ontario: Prentice Hall.
Fowler, N. (1979). *After the riots*. London: Davis-Paynter.
Franks, C. E. S. (1989). *Dissent and the state*. Toronto: Oxford University Press.
Frenkel-Brunswik, E. (1952). Interaction of psychological and sociological factors in
    political behavior. *American Political Science Review, 46*(1), 44-65.
Fricker, M., & Pizzo, S. (1992, May/June). Outlaws at Justice. *Mother Jones,* pp. 30-38.
Fridell, L. (1985). Justifiable use of measures in research on deadly force. *Journal of
    Criminal Justice, 17*(3), 157-166.
Friedrichs, D. O. (1995). State crime or governmental crime: Making sense of the con-
    ceptual confusion. In J. I. Ross (Ed.), *Controlling state crime* (pp. 53-79). New York:
    Garland.
Friedrichs, D. O. (1996). *Trusted criminals: White collar crime in contemporary
    society*. New York: Wadsworth.
Friedrichs, D. O. (1998a). *State crime* (Vol. 1). Aldershot, UK: Ashgate.
Friedrichs, D. O. (1998b). *State crime* (Vol. 2). Aldershot, UK: Ashgate.
Fyfe, J. (1978). *Shots fired: An analysis of New York City firearms discharge*. Unpublished
    doctoral dissertation, State University of New York at Albany.
Fyfe, J. (1979). Administrative interventions on police shooting discretion. *Journal of
    Criminal Justice, 1,* 309-323.
Gamson, W. (1968). *Power and discontent*. Homewood, IL: Dorsey.
Garber, M., & Walkowitz, R. (Eds.). (1995). *Secret agents: The Rosenberg case,
    McCarthyism & fifties America*. New York & London: Routledge.

Gaventa, J. (1980). *Power and powerlessness*. Urbana: University of Illinois Press.

Geary, R. (1985). *Policing industrial disputes: 1893 to 1985*. Cambridge, UK: Cambridge University Press.

Geller, W. A. (1982). Deadly force: What we know. *Journal of Police Science and Administration, 10*, 151-177.

Gibbons, D. C. (1987). *Society, crime, and criminal behavior*. Englewood Cliffs, NJ: Prentice Hall.

Gill, P. (1995). Controlling state crimes by national security agencies. In J. I. Ross (Ed.), *Controlling state crime: An introduction* (pp. 81-114). New York: Garland.

Goldstein, J. S. (1996). *International relations* (2nd ed.). New York: Addison-Wesley Longman.

Goldstein, R. J. (1978). *Political repression in modern America*. Cambridge, MA: Schenkman.

Grabosky, P. N. (1989). *Wayward governance: Illegality and its control in the public sector*. Canberra: Australian Institute of Criminology.

Grace, E., & Leys, C. (1989). The concept of subversion and its implications. In C. E. S. Franks (Ed.), *Dissent and the state* (pp. 62-85). Toronto: Oxford University Press.

Green, G. S. (1990). *Occupational crime*. Chicago: Nelson-Hall.

Greider, W. (1992). *Who will tell the people: The betrayal of American democracy*. New York: Simon and Schuster.

Grosman, B. A. (1972). Political crime and emergency measures in Canada. In F. Adler & G. O. W. Mueller (Eds.), *Politics, crime and the American scene* (pp. 141-146). San Juan, Puerto Rico: North-South Center Press.

Gross, F. (1972). *Violence in politics: Terror and political assassination in Eastern Europe and Russia*. The Hague: Mouton.

Gurr, T. R. (1970). *Why men rebel*. Princeton, NJ: Princeton University Press.

Gurr, T. R. (1988). War, revolution and the growth of the coercive state. *Comparative Political Studies, 21*(1), 45-65.

Gutmann, D. (1979). Killers and consumers: The terrorist and his audience. *Social Research, 46*, 516-526.

Habermas, J. (1975). *Legitimation crisis*. Boston: Beacon.

Hacker, F. J. (1976). *Crusaders, criminals, and crazies: Terror and terrorism in our time*. New York: Norton.

Hagan, F. (1990). *Introduction to criminology: Theories, methods, and criminal behavior*. Chicago: Nelson-Hall

Hagan, F. (1994). *Introduction to criminology: Theories, methods, and criminal behavior* (3rd ed.). Chicago: Nelson Hall.

Hagan, F. (1997). *Political crime: Ideology & criminality*. Boston: Allyn and Bacon.

Hahn, H., & Feagin, J. R. (1970). Riot-precipitating police practices: Attitudes in urban ghettos. *Phylon, 31*, 183-193.

Haldeman, H. R. (1994). *The Haldeman diaries: Inside the Nixon White House*. New York: Simon and Schuster.

Halperin, M., Burosage, R. I., & Marwick, C. M. (1977). *The lawless state: The crimes of the U.S. intelligence agencies*. New York: Penguin.

Hamilton, L. C. (1978). *Ecology of terrorism: A historical and statistical study*. Unpublished doctoral dissertation, University of Colorado.

Hamm, M. S. (1995). *The abandoned ones: The imprisonment and uprising of the Mariel boat people*. Boston: Northeastern University Press.

Haritos-Fatouros, M. (1988). The official torturer: A learning model for obedience to the authority of violence. *Journal of Applied Social Psychology, 18*, 1107-1120.

Harring, S. (1983). *Policing a class society*. New Brunswick, NJ: Rutgers University Press.

Havill, A. (2001). *The spy who stayed out in the cold: The secret life of FBI double agent Robert Hanssen*. New York: St. Martin's.

Hazelhurst, K. M. (1991). Passion and policy: Aboriginal deaths in custody in Australia, 1980-1989. In G. Barak (Ed.), *Crimes by the capitalist state* (pp. 21-48). Albany: State University of New York Press.

Henry, S. (1991). The informal economy: A crime of omission by the state. In G. Barak (Ed.), *Crimes by the capitalist state* (pp. 253-272). Albany: State University of New York Press.

Herman, E. (1982). *The real terror network*. Boston: South End.

Herring, G. C. (Ed.). (1993). *The Pentagon papers* (Abridged ed.). New York: McGraw Hill.

Hitchens, C. (2001). *The trial of Henry Kissinger*. London: Verso.

Holtsi, O. R., Brody, R. A., & North, R. C. (1964). Measuring affect and action in international relations models: Empirical materials from the 1962 Cuban crisis. *Journal of Peace Research*, 170-189.

Home Affairs Committee. (1980). *Deaths in custody*. London: HMSO.

Horvath, F. (1987). The police use of deadly force: A description of selected characteristics of intrastate incidents. *Journal of Police Science and Administration, 15*, 26-238.

Hubbard, D. G. (1971). *The skyjacker: His flights of fantasy*. New York: Macmillan.

Hubbard, D. G. (1983). The psychodynamics of terrorism. In Y. Alexander & T. Adeniran (Eds.), *International violence* (pp. 43-53). New York: Praeger.

Hurst, J. W. (1971). Treason. In *Encyclopedia of crime and justice* (pp. 1559-1562). New York: Free Press.

Hurwitz, L. (1995). International state-sponsored organizations to control state crime: The European Convention on Human Rights. In J. I. Ross (Ed.), *Controlling state crime* (pp. 383-315). New York: Garland.

IJOGT. (1982a). Psychology of leaders of terrorist groups. International Scientific Conference on Terror and Terrorism: International Terrorism. *International Journal of Group Tensions, 12*, 84-104.

IJOGT. (1982b). Psychology of the followers. International Scientific Conference on Terror and Terrorism: International Terrorism. *International Journal of Group Tensions, 12*, 105-121.

Information. (2002). Human Rights Watch. Retrieved June 8, 2002, from http://www. hrw.org/about/info/qna.html

Ingelhart, R. (1977). *Silent revolution*. Princeton, NJ: Princeton University Press.

Ingraham, B. L. (1979). *Political crime in Europe: A comparative England*. Berkeley: University of California Press.

Ingraham, B. L., & Tokoro, K. (1969). Political crime in the United States and Japan. *Issues in Criminology, 4*(2), 145-169.

Jenkins, B. (1982). *Terrorism and beyond: An international conference on terrorism and low level conflict*. Santa Monica, CA: RAND.

Jenkins, P. (1988). Whose terrorists? Libya and state criminality. *Contemporary Crises, 12,* 1-11.

Johnson, C. (1982). *Revolutionary change*. Stanford, CA: Stanford University Press.

Johnson, R., & Leighton, P. (1999). American genocide: The destruction of the black underclass. In C. Summers & E. Markusen (Eds.), *Collective violence: Harmful behavior in groups and governments* (pp. 95-140). Lantham, MD: Rowman and Littlefield.

Jongman, A. J. (1983). A world directory of "terrorist" organizations and other groups, movements and parties involved in political violence as initiators or targets of armed violence. In A. P. Schmid (Ed.), *Political terrorism: A research guide to concepts, theories, data bases and literature* (pp. 284-417). New Brunswick, NJ: Transaction Books.

Joseph, J. (1994). *Signs of life: Channel surfing through 90s culture*. San Francisco: Manic D Press.

Kania, R. E., & Mackay, W. C. (1977). Police violence as a function of community characteristics. *Criminology, 15,* 27-48.

Kaplan, A. (1978). The psychodynamics of terrorism. *Terrorism: An International Journal, 1,* 237-254.

Kappeler, V. E., Sluder, R. D., & Alpert, G. P. (1994). *Forces of deviance*. Prospect Heights, IL: Waveland.

Kasinitz, P. (1983). Neo-Marxist views of the state. *Dissent, 30,* 337-346.

Kauzlarich, D., & Kramer, R. C. (1993). State-corporate crime in the U.S. nuclear weapons production complex. *Journal of Human Justice, 5,* 4-28.

Kauzlarich, D., & Kramer, R. C. (1998). *Crimes of the American nuclear state*. Boston: Northeastern University Press.

Keenan, J. P. (1987). *A new perspective on terrorism: Theories and hypotheses*. A paper presented at the annual meeting of the American Society of Criminology, Montreal.

Kelly, R. J. (1972). New political crimes and the emergence of revolutionary national-ist ideologies. In F. Adler & G. O. W. Mueller (Eds.), *Politics, crime and the international scene: An inter-American focus* (pp. 23-35). San Juan, Puerto Rico: North-South Center Press.

Kelman, H. (1983). Conversations with Arafat. *American Psychologist, 70,* 203-216.

Kettle, M., & Hodges, L. (1982). *Uprising! The police, the people and the riots in Britain's cities*. London: Pan Books.

Khan, R. A., & McNiven, J. D. (1991). *An introduction to political science* (4th ed.). Scarborough, Ontario: Nelson Canada.

Kirchheimer, O. (1961). *Political justice: The use of legal procedure for political ends.* Princeton, NJ: Princeton University Press.

Kittrie, N. N. (1972). International law and political crime. In F. Adler & G. O. W. Mueller (Eds.), *Politics, crime and the international scene: An inter-American focus* (pp. 91-95). San Juan, Puerto Rico: North-South Centre Press.

Kittrie, N. N. (2000). *Rebels with a cause.* Boulder, CO: Westview.

Kittrie, N. N., & Wedlock, E. D., Jr. (1986). *The tree of liberty: A documentary history of rebellion and political crime in America.* Baltimore MD: Johns Hopkins University Press.

Kneece, J. (1986). *Family treason: The Walker spy ring case.* New York: Stein and Day.

Knutson, J. (1981). Social and psychodynamic pressures toward a negative identity: The case of an American revolutionary terrorist. In Y. Alexander & J. M. Gleason (Eds.), *Behavioral and quantitative perspectives on terrorism* (pp. 105-152). Toronto: Pergamon.

Kohn, S. M. (1994). *American political prisoners: Prosecutions under the Espionage and Sedition Acts.* Westport, CT: Praeger.

Koistra, P. G. (1985, March). What is a political crime? *Criminal Justice Abstracts, 17,* pp. 100-115.

Kramer, R. C. (1982). Corporate crime: An organizational perspective. In P. Wickman & T. Dailey (Eds.), *White-collar and economic crime* (pp. 75-94). Lexington, MA: Lexington Books.

Kramer, R. C. (1992). The Space Shuttle Challenger explosion: A case study of state-corporate crime. In K. Schlegel & D. Weisburd (Eds.), *White-collar crime reconsidered* (pp. 214-243). Boston: Northeastern University Press.

Kramer, R. C., & Michalowski, R. J. (1990). *State-corporate crime.* Paper presented at the annual meeting of the American Society of Criminology, Baltimore, MD.

Kuper, L. (1985). *The prevention of genocide.* New Haven, CT: Yale University Press.

Laqueur, W. (1977). *Terrorism.* Boston: Little, Brown.

Laqueur, W. (1985). *A world of secrets.* New York: Twentieth Century Fund.

Lichbach, M. (1987). Deterrence or escalation: The puzzle of aggregate studies of repression and dissent. *Journal of Conflict Resolution, 31*(2), 266-297.

Lukes, S. (1974). *Power: A radical view.* London: Macmillan.

Maas, P. (1973). *Serpico.* New York: Viking.

Manheim, J. B., & Rich, R. C. (1986). *Empirical political analysis.* New York: Longman.

Manning, P. K. (1980). Violence and the police role. *Annals of the American Academy of Political and Social Science, 452,* 135-144.

Manning, P. K. (1991). The police. In J. F. Sheley (Ed.), *Criminology* (pp. 337-357). Belmont, CA: Wadsworth.

Mannle, H. W., & Hirschel, J. D. (1988). *Fundamentals of criminology* (2nd ed.). Englewood Cliffs, NJ: Prentice Hall.

Marchetti, V., & Marks, J. D. (1975). *The CIA and the cult of intelligence.* New York: Dell.

Margolin, J. (1977). Psychological perspectives in terrorism. In Y. Alexander & S. M. Finger (Eds.), *Terrorism: Interdisciplinary perspectives* (pp. 270-282). New York: John Jay Press.

Markovitz, A. S., & Silverstein, M. (Eds.). (1988). *The politics of scandal*. New York: Holmes and Meire.

Marshall, J., Scott, P. D., & Hunter, J. (1987). *The Iran-Contra connection: Secret teams and covert operations in the Reagan era*. Boston: South End.

Martin, B. (1995). Eliminating state crime by abolishing the state. In J. I. Ross (Ed.), *Controlling state crime* (pp. 389-417). New York: Garland.

Marx, G. T. (1970a). Civil disorder and agents of social control. *Journal of Social Issues, 26,* 19-57.

Marx, G. T. (1970b). Issueless riots. *Annals of the American Academy of Political and Social Science, 39,* 21-33.

Marx, G. T. (1988). *Undercover: Police surveillance in America*. Berkeley: University of California Press.

Marx, K., & Engels, F. (1848). *The Communist manifesto*. New York: International Publishers.

Matthews, R., & Kauzlarich, D. (2000). The crash of ValuJet flight 592: A case study in state-corporate crime. *Sociological Focus, 3,* 281-298.

Matthiesen, P. (1991). *In the spirit of Crazy Horse*. New York: Penguin.

McCauley, C. R., & Segal, M. E. (1987). Social psychology of terrorist groups. In C. Hendrick (Ed.), *Annual review of social and personality psychology: Group processes and intergroup relation* (pp. 231-256). Newbury Park, CA: Sage.

Merton, R. K. (1938). Social structure and anomie. *American Sociological Review, 3,* 672-682.

Merton, R. K. (1964). Anomie, anomia, and social interaction: Contexts of deviant behavior. In M. B. Clinard (Ed.), *Anomie and deviant behavior*. New York: Free Press.

Merton, R. K. (1966). Social problems and sociological theory. In R. K. Merton & R. A. Nisbet (Eds.), *Contemporary social problems*. New York: Harcourt Brace.

Michalowski, R. J. (1985). *Order, law, and crime*. New York: Random House.

Mickolus, E. (1981). *Combatting international terrorism: A quantitative approach*. Unpublished doctoral dissertation, Yale University.

Miligram, S. (1974). *Obedience to authority*. London: Harper and Row.

Miligram, S. (1977). *The individual and the social world*. Boston, MA: Addison-Wesley.

Miller, R. R. (2000). Controlling state crime in Israel: The dichotomy between national security versus coercive powers. In J. I. Ross (Ed.), *Varieties of state crime and its control* (pp. 89-118). Monsey, NY: Criminal Justice Press.

Millett, K. (1994). *The politics of cruelty: An essay on the literature of political imprisonment*. New York: Norton.

Mills, C. W. (1956). *The power elite*. New York: Oxford University Press.

Miron, M. S. (1976). Psycholinguistic analysis of the SLA. *Assets Protection, 1,* 14-19.

Mitchell, C., Stohl, M., Carleton, D., & Lopez, G. A. (1986). State terrorism: Issues of concept and measurement. In M. Stohl & G. A. Lopez (Eds.), *Government violence and repression* (pp. 1-26). Westport, CT: Greenwood.

Mitchell, T. H. (1985). *Politically-motivated terrorism in North America: The threat and the response.* Unpublished doctoral dissertation, Carleton University.

Morf, G. (1970). *Terror in Québec.* Toronto: Clarke, Irwin.

Morn, R. (1974). *Political crime.* Unpublished doctoral dissertation, University of Pennsylvania.

Navanksy, V. (1991). *Naming names.* New York: Viking Penguin

Neville, J. F. (1995). *Press, the Rosenberg's & the Cold War.* Greenwood, CT: Greenwood.

Noonan, J. (1984). *Bribes.* New York: Macmillan.

Nye, J., Jr., Zelikow, P., & King, D. C. (1997). *Why people don't trust the government.* Cambridge, MA: Harvard University Press.

Packer, H. L. (1962). Offenses against the state. *The Annals of the American Academy, 339,* 77-89.

Parenti, M. (1995). *Democracy for the few* (2nd ed.). New York: St. Martin's.

Pearce, F. (1976). *Crimes of the powerful.* London: Pluto.

Pearce, F., & Tombs, S. (1998). *Toxic capitalism: Corporate crime and the chemical industry.* Brookfield, VT: Ashgate.

Pearlstein, R. M. (1991). *The mind of a political terrorist.* Wilmington, DE: Scholarly Resources.

Pitcher, B., & Hamblin, R. (1982). Collective learning in ongoing political conflicts. *International Political Science Review, 3,* 71-90.

Pollis, A., & Schwab, P. (1979). Human rights: A Western construct with limited applicability. In A. Pollis & P. Schwab (Eds.), Human rights: Cultural and ideological perspectives (pp. 1-18). New York: Praeger.

Polsby, N. (1980). *Community power and political theory* (Rev. ed.). New Haven, CT: Yale University Press.

Post, J. M. (1986). Hostilité, conformité, fraternité: The group dynamics of terrorist behavior. *International Journal of Group Psychotherapy, 36,* 211-224.

Post, J. M. (1990). Terrorist psycho-logic: Terrorist behavior as a product of psychological forces. In W. Reich (Ed.), *Origins of terrorism* (pp. 25-40). Cambridge, UK: Cambridge University Press.

Poulantzas, N. (1973). *Political power and social classes.* London: Verso.

Power, J. (1981). *Amnesty International: The human rights story.* New York: McGraw-Hill.

Proal, L. (1973). *Political crime* (Reprint ed.). Montclair, NJ: Paterson Smith. (Original work published 1898)

Quinney, R. (1970). *The social reality of crime.* Boston: Little, Brown.

Quinney, R. (1974). *Critique of legal order: Crime control in capitalist society.* Boston: Little, Brown.

Quinney, R. (1977). *Class, state, and crime.* New York: David McKay.

Ranelagh, J. (1987). *The Agency: The rise and decline of the CIA* (Revised & updated). New York: Simon and Schuster.

Ratner, R. S., & McMullen, J. (1983). Social control and the rise of the "exceptional state" in Britain, the United States and Canada. *Crime and Social Justice, 19,* 31-43.

Redden, J. (2000). *Snitch culture: How citizens are turned into the eyes and ears of the state*. Venice, CA: Feral House.

Reeve, S. (1999). *The new jackals*. Boston: Northeastern University Press.

Reich, W. (1990). Understanding terrorist behavior: The limits and opportunities of psychological inquiry. In W. Reich (Ed.), *Origins of terrorism* (pp. 261-281). Cambridge, UK: Cambridge University Press.

Reilly, W. G. (1973). Canada, Québec and theories of internal war. *American Review of Canadian Studies, 3*, 67-75.

Reiman, J. (1998). *The rich get richer and the poor get prison* (5th ed.). Boston: Allyn and Bacon.

Reiner, R. (1980). Forces of disorder: How the police control "riots." *New Society, 10*, 51-54.

Reiss, A. J., Jr. (1968). Police brutality: Answers to key questions. *Trans-Action, 10*, 19.

Richards, S. C., & Avey, M. (2000). Controlling state crime in the United States of America: What can we do about the thug state? In J. I. Ross (Ed.), *Varieties of state crime and its control* (pp. 31-57). Monsey, NY: Criminal Justice Press.

Roberg, R. R., & Kuykendall, J. L. (1993). *Police and society*. Belmont, CA: Wadsworth.

Roberts, A. (1976). The British armed forces and politics: A historical perspective. In C. Enloe & U. Semin-Panzer (Eds.), *Military, the police and domestic order*. London: Richardson Institute for Conflict and Peace Research.

Robertson, G. (2000). *Crimes against humanity: The struggle for global justice*. New York: New Press.

Roebuck, J., & Weeber, S. C. (1978). *Political crime in the United States*. New York: Praeger.

Romano, A. T. (1984). *Terrorism: An analysis of the literature*. Unpublished doctoral dissertation, Fordham University.

Ross, J. I. (1988a). Attributes of political terrorism in Canada, 1960-1985. *Terrorism: An International Journal, 11*(3), 213-233.

Ross, J. I. (1988b). An events data base on political terrorism in Canada: Some conceptual and methodological problems. *Conflict Quarterly, 8*(2), 47-65.

Ross, J. I. (1991). The nature of contemporary international terrorism. In D. Charters (Ed.), *Democratic responses to terrorism* (pp. 17-42). Ardsley-on-Hudson, NY: Transnational Publishers.

Ross, J. I. (1992). Review of Gregg Barak's *Crimes by the capitalist State*. *Justice Quarterly, 9*, 347-354.

Ross, J. I. (1993a). Research on contemporary oppositional political terrorism in the United States: Merits, drawbacks, and suggestions for improvement. In K. D. Tunnell (Ed.), *Political crime in contemporary America: A critical approach* (pp. 101-120). New York: Garland.

Ross, J. I. (1993b). Structural causes of oppositional political terrorism: Towards a causal model. *Journal of Peace Research, 30*(3), 317-329.

Ross, J. I. (1994). The psychological causes of oppositional political terrorism: Toward an integration of findings. *International Journal of Group Tensions, 24*(2), 157-185.

Ross, J. I. (1995/2000). *Controlling state crime* (2nd ed.). New Brunswick, NJ: Transaction Books.

Ross, J. I. (1995a). Controlling state crime: Toward an integrated structural model. In J. I. Ross (Ed.), *Controlling state crime: An introduction* (pp. 3-33). New York: Garland.

Ross, J. I. (1995b). Police violence in Canada. In J. I. Ross (Ed.), *Violence in Canada: Sociopolitical perspectives* (pp. 223-251). Don Mills, Ontario: Oxford University Press.

Ross, J. I. (1995c). The rise and fall of Québécois separatist terrorism: A qualitative application of factors from two models. *Studies in Conflict and Terrorism, 18*(4), 285-297.

Ross, J. I. (Ed.). (1995d). *Violence in Canada: Sociopolitical perspectives*. Don Mills, Ontario: Oxford University Press.

Ross, J. I. (1996). A model of the psychological causes of oppositional political terrorism. *Peace and Conflict: Journal of Peace Psychology, 2*(2), 129-141.

Ross, J. I. (Ed.). (1998a). *Cutting the edge: Current perspectives on radical/critical criminology and criminal justice*. Greenwood, CT: Praeger.

Ross, J. I. (1998b). Radical and critical criminology's treatment of municipal policing. In J. I. Ross (Ed.), *Cutting the edge: Current perspectives on radical/critical criminology and criminal justice* (pp. 95-106). Greenwood, CT: Praeger.

Ross, J. I. (1999). Beyond the conceptualization of terrorism. In C. Summers & E. Markusen (Eds.), *Collective violence: Harmful behavior in groups and governments* (pp. 169-192). Lantham, MD: Rowman and Littlefield.

Ross, J. I. (2000a). Controlling state crime in the United Kingdom. In J. I. Ross (Ed.), *Varieties of state crime and its control* (pp. 11-30). Monsey, NY: Criminal Justice Press.

Ross, J. I. (Ed.). (2000b). *Making news of police violence: Comparing Toronto and New York City*. Greenwood, CT: Praeger.

Ross, J. I. (Ed.). (2000c). *Varieties of state crime and its control*. Monsey, NY: Criminal Justice Press.

Ross, J. I. (2001). Police crime & democracy: Demystifying the concept, research and presenting a taxonomy. In S. Einstein & M. Amir (Eds.), *Policing, security and democracy: Special aspects of "democratic policing"* (pp. 177-200). Huntsville, TX: Office of International Criminal Justice.

Ross, J. I., Barak, G., Kauzlarich, D., Hamm, S., Friedrichs, D., Matthews, R., Pickering, S., Presdee, M., Kraska, P., & Kappeler, V. (1999). The state of state crime research. *Humanity and Society, 23*(3), 273-281.

Ross, J. I., & Gurr, T. R. (1989). Why terrorism subsides: A comparative study of Canada and the United States. *Comparative Politics, 21,* 406-426.

Ross, J. I., & Richards, S. C. (2002). *Behind bars: Surviving prison*. Indianapolis, IN: Alpha Books.

Rothmiller, M., & Goldman, I. G. (1992). *L.A. secret police: Inside the LAPD elite spy network*. New York: Pocket Books.

Russell, C. A., & Miller, B. H. (1983). Profile of a terrorist. In L. Z. Freedman & Y. Alexander (Eds.), *Perspectives on terrorism* (pp. 45-60). Wilmington, DE: Scholarly Resources.

Sabotage. (2002). Retrieved June 5, 2002, from http://www.allwords.com

Sagarin, E. (1973). Introduction. In L. Proal, *Political crime* (Reprint ed., pp. v-xvi). Montclair, NJ: Paterson Smith.

Saltstone, S. P. (1991). Some consequences of the failure to define the phrase "national security." *Conflict Quarterly, 11*(3), 36-54.

Sawatsky, J. (1980). *Men in the shadows: The RCMP Security Service.* Toronto: Doubleday.

Sawatsky, J. (1984). *Gouzenko: The untold story.* Toronto: Macmillan.

Sayari, S. (1985). *Generational change in terrorist movements: The Turkish case.* Santa Monica, CA: RAND.

Schafer, S. (1971). The concept of the political criminal. *Journal of Criminal Law, Criminology, and Police Science,* 62(3), pp. 380-387.

Schafer, S. (1974). *The political criminal.* New York: Free Press.

Scharf, P., & Binder, A. (1983). *The badge and the bullet: Police use of deadly force.* New York: Praeger.

Scheingold, S. (1998). Constructing the new political criminology: Power, authority, and the post-liberal state. *Law and Social Inquiry, 23*(4), pp. 857-895.

Schenck v. United States (249 U.S. 47), 1919.

Schmalleger, F. (2002). *Criminal law today.* Upper Saddle River, NJ: Prentice Hall.

Schmid, A. (1983). *Political terrorism: A guide to concepts, theories, data bases and literature.* New Brunswick, NJ: Transaction Books.

Schmid, A. (1988). *Political terrorism: A new guide to actors, authors, concepts, data bases, theories and literature.* Amsterdam: SWIDOC/Transaction.

Schwendinger, H., & Schwendinger, J. (1975). Defenders of order or guardians of human rights? In I. Taylor, P. Walton, & J. Young (Eds.), *Critical criminology* (pp. 113-146). London: Routledge & Kegan Paul.

Scraton, P. (1985). *The state of the police.* London: Pluto.

Scraton, P., & Chadwick, K. (1985). *In the arms of the law: Deaths in custody.* London: Cobden Trust.

Senate Select Committee on Intelligence. (1989). *The FBI and CISPES.* 101st Congress, 1st session, July, Committee Print: 1.

Shank, Greg (Ed.). (1980). State and corporate crime: An introduction. *Social Justice, 16*(2), i-vi.

Sharkansky, I. (1995). A state action may be nasty but it is not likely to be a crime. In J. I. Ross (Ed.), *Controlling state crime* (pp. 35-52). New York: Garland.

Sherman, A. (1978). *Scandal and reform: Controlling police corruption.* Berkeley: University of California Press.

Sherman, L. W. (1980a). Executions without trial. *Vanderbilt Law Review, 33,* 71-100.

Sherman, L. W. (1980b). Perspectives on police and violence. *Annals of the American Academy of Political and Social Science, 452,* 1-12.

Simon, D., & Eitzen, D. S. (1999). *Elite deviance* (6th ed.). Boston: Allen and Bacon.

Simon, H. (1982). *Models of bounded rationality.* Cambridge, MA: MIT Press.

Skocpol, T. (1979). *States and social revolution*. Cambridge, MA: Harvard University Press.

Snepp, F. (1977). *Decent interval: An insider's account of Saigon's indecent end*. New York: Random House.

Snepp, F. (1999). *Irreparable harm: A firsthand account of how one agent took on the CIA in an epic battle*. New York: Random House.

Spjut, R. J. (1974). Defining subversion. *British Journal of Law and Society, 6*(2), 254-261.

Stark, R. (1972). *Police riots*. Belmont, CA: Wadsworth.

Sterling, C. (1981). *The terror network*. New York: Holt, Rinehart and Winston.

Stone, G. R. (1983). Sedition. In *Encyclopedia of crime and justice* (pp. 1425-1431). New York: Free Press.

Sutherland, D. (1980). *The fourth man: The definitive story of Blunt, Philby, Burgess, and Maclean*. London: Sacker & Warburg.

Sutherland, E. H. (1947). *Principles of criminology* (4th ed.). Philadelphia: J. B. Lippincott.

Sutherland, E. H. (1949a). *White collar crime*. New York: Holt, Rinehart and Winston.

Sutherland, E. H. (1949b). The white collar criminal. In V. C. Branham & S. B. Kutash (Eds.), *Encyclopedia of criminology* (pp. 511-515). New York: Philosophical Library.

Sykes, G. M. (1980). *The future of crime*. Rockville, MD: National Institute of Mental Health.

Sykes, G. M., & Cullen, F. (1992). *Criminology* (2nd ed.). Toronto: Harcourt Brace Jovanovich.

Sykes, G. M., & Matza, D. (1957). Techniques of neutralization: A theory of delinquency. *American Sociological Review, 22*, 667-670.

Taft, P., & Ross, P. (1979). American labor violence: Its causes, character, and outcome. In H. D. Graham & T. R. Gurr (Eds.), *Violence in America: Historical & comparative perspectives* (pp. 187-242). Beverly Hills, CA: Sage.

Targ, H. R. (1979). Societal structure and revolutionary terrorism: A preliminary investigation. In M. Stohl (Ed.), *The politics of terrorism* (pp. 119-143). New York: Marcel Dekker.

Taylor, M. (1988). *The terrorist*. London: Brassey's Defence Publishers.

Theoharis, A. (1978). *Spying on Americans: Political surveillance from Hoover to the Huston Plan*. Philadelphia: Temple University Press.

Thomas, C. W., & Hepburn, J. R. (1983). *Crime, criminal law, and criminology*. Dubuque, IA: William C. Brown.

Thomas, D. S. (Ed.). (1972). *Treason and libel*. Boston: Routledge and Kegan Paul.

Thornton, T. P. (1964). Terror as a weapon of political agitation. In H. Eckstein (Ed.), *Internal war: Problems and approaches* (pp. 82-88). New York: Free Press of Glencoe.

Thurlow, R. (1994). *The secret state: British internal security in the twentieth century*. Cambridge, MA: Blackwell.

Tilly, C. (1978). *From mobilization to revolution*. Reading, MA: Addison-Wesley.

Tilly, C. (1985). War making and state making as organized crime. In P. B. Evans, D. Rueschemeyer, & T. Skocpol (Eds.), *Bringing the state back in*. Cambridge, UK: Cambridge University Press.

Torrance, J. (1977). The response of Canadian governments to violence. *Canadian Journal of Political Science, 10*, 473-496.

Torrance, J. (1995). The responses of democratic governments to violence. In J. I. Ross (Ed.), *Violence in Canada: Sociopolitical perspectives* (pp. 313-343). Toronto: Oxford University Press.

Tunnell, K. D. (1992). *Choosing crime: The criminal calculus of property offenders*. Chicago: Nelson-Hall.

Tunnell, K. D. (1993a). Political crime and pedagogy: A content analysis of criminology and criminal justice texts, *Journal of Criminal Justice Education, 4*(1), 101-114.

Tunnell, K. D. (Ed.). (1993b). *Political crime in contemporary America: A critical approach*. New York: Garland.

Tunnell, K. D. (1995a). Crimes of the capitalist state against labor. In J. I. Ross (Ed.), *Controlling state crime* (pp. 207-233). New York: Garland.

Tunnell, K. D. (1995b). Worker insurgency and social control: Violence by and against labor in Canada. In J. I. Ross (Ed.), *Violence in Canada* (pp. 78-96). Toronto: Oxford University Press.

Turk, A. T. (1982a). *Political criminality*. Beverly Hills, CA: Sage.

Turk, A. T. (1982b). Social dynamics of terrorism. *Annals of the American Association of Political and Social Sciences, 463*, 119-128.

Turk, A. T. (1984). Political crime. In R. F. Meir (Ed.), *Major forms of crime* (pp. 119-135). Beverly Hills, CA: Sage.

U.S. Department of State. (2002). Retrieved June 8, 2002, from www.state.gov/g/drl/rls/hrrpt/2000/wha/index.cfm?docid=729

Van Maanen, J. (1973). Observations on the making of policemen. *Human Organization, 32*, 407-418.

Vaughn, D. (1996). *The* Challenger *launch decision*. Chicago: University of Chicago Press.

Vetter, H., & Perlstein, G. R. (1991). *Perspectives on terrorism*. Pacific Grove, CA: Brooks/Cole.

Wardlaw, G. (1982). *Political terrorism*. Cambridge, UK: Cambridge University Press.

Warr, M. (1995). Public perceptions of crime and punishment. In J. F. Sheley (Ed.), *Criminology* (2nd ed., pp. 15-31). Belmont, CA: Wadsworth.

Webster's new collegiate dictionary. (1980). Toronto: Thomas Allen & Son.

Weinberg, L., & Davis, P. B. (1989). *Introduction to political terrorism*. New York: McGraw-Hill.

Weinberg, L., & Eubank, W. L. (1987). Italian women terrorists. *Terrorism: An International Journal, 9*, 241-262.

Welch, M. (1996). *Corrections: A critical approach*. New York: McGraw-Hill.

Westley, W. A. (1953). Violence and the police. *American Journal of Sociology, 59*, 34-41.

Westley, W. A. (1970). *Violence and the police: A sociological study of law, custom and morality*. Cambridge, MA: MIT Press.

Wexley, J. (1977). *The judgment of Julius and Ethel Rosenberg*. New York: Ballantine.

Whyte, J. D., & MacDonald, A. (1989). Dissent and national security and dissent some more. In C. E. S. Franks (Ed.), *Dissent and the state* (pp. 21-39). Toronto: Oxford University Press.

Williams, M. (1991, September 30-October 6). Getting a grip (or losing it) on Iran-Contra. *Washington Post*, pp. 11-12.

Wolfe, A. (1973). *The seamy side of democracy: Repression in America*. New York: David McKay.

Woodward, B. (1987). *Veil: The secret wars of the CIA 1981-1987*. New York: Pocket Books.

Woodward, B., & Bernstein, C. (1974). *All the president's men*. New York: Simon and Schuster.

Worden, R. E. (1995). The "causes" of police brutality: Theory and evidence on police use of force. In W. A. Geller & H. Toch (Eds.), *And justice for all* (pp. 31-60). Washington, DC: Police Executive Research Forum.

Wright, J. P., Cullen, F. T., & Blankenship, M. B. (1995). The social construction of corporate violence: Media coverage of the Imperial Food Products fire. *Crime and Delinquency, 41,* 20-36.

Wright, S. (1998). *An appraisal of technologies of political control*. Report to the European Parliament, January 6, Luxembourg.

Zwerman, G. (1988). Domestic counter terrorism. *Social Justice, 16,* 31-63.

ANSWERS TO MULTIPLE-CHOICE QUESTIONS

CHAPTER 1

1. e
2. e
3. e
4. e
5. d
6. d
7. a

CHAPTER 2

1. e
2. e
3. b
4. c
5. b
6. c
7. d

CHAPTER 3

1. c
2. a
3. c
4. d
5. a
6. b
7. e

CHAPTER 4

1. e
2. c
3. e
4. b
5. b
6. e
7. b

CHAPTER 5

1. c
2. d
3. a
4. d
5. c
6. b
7. c

CHAPTER 6

1. a
2. e
3. e
4. c
5. a
6. e
7. d

CHAPTER 7

1. c
2. d
3. a
4. d
5. a
6. b
7. e

CHAPTER 8

1. b
2. e
3. d
4. b
5. a
6. b
7. a

CHAPTER 9

1. d
2. b
3. e
4. a
5. e
6. c
7. a

CHAPTER 10

1. d
2. d
3. d
4. b
5. b
6. c
7. c

CHAPTER 11

1. c
2. b
3. a
4. b
5. d
6. d
7. d

CHAPTER 12

1. a
2. b
3. b
4. e
5. b
6. d
7. c

INDEX

ABOUT THE AUTHOR

Jeffrey Ian Ross, Ph.D., is Assistant Professor, Division of Criminology, Criminal Justice, and Social Policy, and a Research Fellow at the Center for Comparative and International Law at the University of Baltimore. He has conducted research, written, and lectured on national security, political and criminal violence, political crime, policing, and corrections for more than 15 years. His work has appeared in many academic journals and books, as well as in popular magazines. He is the author of *Making News of Police Violence* (2000), coauthor (with Stephen C. Richards) of *Behind Bars: Surviving Prison* (2002), editor of *Controlling State Crime* (2nd ed., 2000), *Violence in Canada: Sociopolitical Perspectives* (1995), *Cutting the Edge: Current Perspectives in Radical/Critical Criminology and Criminal Justice* (1998), *Varieties of State Crime and Its Control* (2000), and the coeditor (with Stephen C. Richards) of *Convict Criminology* (2002). In 1986, Ross was the lead expert witness for the Senate of Canada's Special Committee on Terrorism and Public Safety. He received his Ph.D. in political science from the University of Colorado and was a Social Science Analyst with the National Institute of Justice, a division of the U.S. Department of Justice, before coming to the University of Baltimore.

This book is dedicated to Austin T. Turk, mentor and colleague, who introduced me to the academic field of criminology and criminal justice, and who taught me that in professional life, theoretical and methodological differences among scholars should be friendly and facilitative.

The DYNAMICS of POLITICAL CRIME

WITHDRAWN